Facing West

Voices of Western Women.

Lynn Brown

A collection by Sally Harper Bates

It must be said … THANK YOU TO

Award winning author, Heidi Thomas, for her
expertise and constant support in the editing and
production of this book.

Marless Fellows for the painting
used on the cover.
Steve Atkinson for his graphic artistry that made
the cover spring to life.

To Mike Capron and Lynn Brown for allowing
use of their drawings to brighten up the pages.

To Nika Nordbrock for her editing and critique.

*And, of course, all the writers who responded to
my call to share their work in these pages. It is
obvious this book would never have come to
fruition if not for their generosity and talent.*

Pen & Ink by Roni Harper

Out where the hand-clasp's a little stronger,

out where the smiles last a little longer…

that's where the West begins.

Arthur Chapman

The West is fine for men and cattle,

but the West is hell on horses and women.

Unknown

INTRODUCTION

In the movie *Australia*, we hear the voice of a young man saying his grandfather taught him that telling stories is how we keep people with us. I believe that whole-heartedly. And whether you're a "good storyteller" or not so much, your story is worth telling, and saving, and being. Some of the voices in here are those of published, award winning writers, but most are first-timers. Fresh voices, having limited exposure or publication of their work.

Time moves forward and never looks back. It is our memories that have the ability to bring back, to re-live, to keep alive. If we will find or make time to tell them, to write them, or to record them.

One of the precious facets of what lies within the voices of these women is the re-living of life. Keeping it breathing. Keeping it from growing stale and forgotten. For when we, as sisters, sit and talk, remember, dream together, we hold time and life in our hearts and hands for a moment again. It is there we will find our fathers and grandfathers. Mothers and grandmothers. Sisters and aunts. Their names will be spoken; their lives remembered; their deeds recorded. With them, we will find a sense of our own immortality.

The pages of this book hold the words of my friends and extended family. The lines and word pictures you will find herein are exemplary of culture, heritage, and traditions. Fears, hopes, dreams, suffering and joy. Life in this West of ours. When I read these lines, I hear the voices of women in our beloved West, telling their story, singing their song, and setting their hearts down on paper.

Sally Harper Bates
Editor & Publisher

FOREWORD

"Cowgirls don't follow trails; they blaze them." This can be said for western ranch women in general.

Since the days of covered wagons and homesteading, women have been the support beam, the guiding light, the "right hand" to their fathers, brothers and husbands. They've worked alongside the men to build a home, a farm, or a ranch, and take care of livestock and crops. They walked behind a plow, picked up rocks, planted gardens and rode horses. Then they chopped wood, milked cows, baked and cooked, washed clothes, and birthed babies.

They've had to improvise and "make-do' - creating a Christmas tree from a dead century plant or a giant sagebrush, sewing dresses from flour sacks, stretching a meal for four into a banquet for unexpected company.

Women were, and still are, cowhands, ranchers, ropers, riders, veterinarians, errand runners, and they wear a multitude of "hats" in order to keep the train running on track. But they are also ladies who enjoy getting dressed up, going to a movie or a dance, and being romanced by their men. They are intellectually curious women who love to read and sing or write poetry and stories about their lives.

Facing West is an insight to ranch life behind the movies and romance novels. The voices in this book are those of the women who build the foundation for their western families.

Heidi Thomas
Co-editor

WHEN THE LAND WAS YOUNG

When the land was young and I was free
And the wind blew me where I would be
My soul would laugh at those who decree
What a man must do, what a man must be
And I washed my face in a spring fed stream
And nursed myself on what pleasured me.

When the land was young and we were free
The earth was all that mastered me
And the starry sky and the milky moon
Were all that mattered much to me
All that would ever keep me free
For men knew not what pleasured me.

When the land was young and I was free
And the sun rising up was what warmed me
And the moon that fell in the western sea
And the stars that roamed above all I could see
Were all the friends I ever would need
And I fed myself on what pleasured me.

When the land was young and I was free
And the golden skies awakened me
I dreamed and roamed where the wind was warm
And the open skies were then my home
I went my way with a swish and song
And always and ever brought pleasure along.

When the land was young and I was free
There just wasn't much that would bother me
But silly boys, and their silly toys
And silly girls with their bouncing curls
Who tossed their hair, to primp and furl.
But only the horses pleasured me.

When the land was young and I was free
I began to roam with the stars and sea
That sea of grass that covered the earth
Swaying with winds that blew through me
Leading me on to where I would be,
To feed on all that pleasured me.

When the land was young and I was free
So long ago, and so yesterly
I lost my way on the grassy sea
And thought the men who dared decree
Would never find or master me,
For they knew not what pleasured me.

When the land was young and I was free
As open as ever the eye could see
The skies were clear, and the air was clean
And not one person I knew was mean
But rather, just wild and free like me
And all we did, was what pleasured me.

Until age and sage became part of me
And nothing at all came easy or free
I wondered the depth, and the heart of me
When life decreed what came to me
And men I knew, who knew not me,
Became the least of what pleasured me.

When I was young, and my heart was free
I danced and sang when it pleasured me
And my heart would soar as I skimmed the floor
And watched as the lights, passed by so bright,
And the music filled my soul to the brim
And I found that was what pleasured me.

When the earth was free, and I was young
I found myself where I belonged

Amid the space of time, and place
In the rocky hills and distant rills
And as I ran and fled what hindered me
I found those things that pleasured me.

Then, the land, still young, but I . . . not free
Did not expose what pleasured me
But held it again, inside my heart
To pray once again I could be a part
Of the cowboy ways, and horseback days
And again those things would pleasure me.

Now the land is older and I'm not free
Nor am I fodder for men that decree
What I must be and what rules me.
For I've a God who watches me
And a Lord who says what I must be
And that . . . is all that pleasures me.

Sally Harper Bates

For my Dad, and others, who gave up that freedom for family.

WE WILL COWBOY

It's more than a job
It's a life recognizable
The way we dress
The crease of our hat
The sun's lasting kiss on our cheek

Our rugged hands scarred by weather and work
Eyes that gaze past you
Seeming to see only distant ridges and canyons
Or cow tracks
Or the prediction of rain in the thunderheads on a summer day

We will cowboy

There are long days and short sleeps out here in big country
An expanse that spreads as far as the eye can see
We stand tall and we ride proud
This is our country
Only for a season
To nurture
To protect
To love and glean a living from
Though none of it may ever bear our name
You'd not know that by our tending

We will cowboy

Raindrops sweet scent on dry thirsty earth
The silence of snowflakes
The smell of a good horse after an honest day's work
The moan of old leather at daylight as we head out
The song of rowels in time with the pace
The fragrance of mountain mahogany
And sage
And cedar carried on the breeze

Mud
And cow

And burning hair
And branding fire
And supper
And life

We will cowboy

Rust and dust are the future's hold for the tangible things we carry
Trinkets of places
And people
Our legacy courses through the veins of our sons and daughters
Those that one day will receive the precious responsibility
Of land
And cow
And cavvy
And a birthright love for open spaces
Long days
Tradition and heritage

We will cowboy

One day we'll look out upon some glorious sunrise with old eyes
And we'll see the silhouettes of our heirs
Men and women born to this
Those who have inherited our strength
Our determination
Our passion for this life
And we'll remember those faded days of cold
And heat
And aching muscles
And we'll know that our legacy is in good hands

And they will cowboy

Mary Matli
with Daron Little and Terry McCall Knight

THERE ARE NO YARD SALES OUT HERE

This place is a living graveyard. Falling down monuments are the unattended shrines to past hopes and dreams under a hazy western sky.

A soggy, partially stuffed pup keeps watch in the yard. His fur is matted and his body is embedded in the dirt. The one ear he has left is cocked and pointed to the dirt road listening for the return of a little girl who has long since grown.

Mama's cactus garden seems petrified in the hard red soil. A strong southern gust exposes a sliver of hopeful green piercing the world from underneath. Her broken broom handle has blown into the yard. Lace curtains, sewn by hand, hang in stillness where she left them in the windows overlooking the corrals in the canyon bottom below. A Bible lays open on a small writing table with hand written notes in the margins. They are artifacts now awaiting interpretation.

Papa's rusted and dusty pipe-fittings and tools fill the old wood ammo boxes from his years of service in the army. It seems he suffered ages to finally hold his cowboy dream in hand. Mama kept his secrets in her heart and bore him up when the long, moonless nights of winter left him too long with his memories.

In the leaning barn, a jewelry box sits on the shelf. The tattered and dingy velvet and satin hold nothing but the dust that has blown in off the dry dirt tank. What dust begat, time forgot, and even that memory is no more.

Hoof-beats forever echo through the empty pens, filling the ears of the on-looker with their deafening silence. Outbuildings are tombs to dreams left unrealized. Someone must have walked away and disappeared into town.

"But this is what I was made for!" Fist held to the sky, tears crashing into the dust kicked high by that old duct taped boot. I feel his anger brush over my heart – a chilling wind.

Was it a bad year? Was the feed grazed off before the rains came? Did the bank leave them with a stack of too much and too little? Did the market crash and leave the owners with no other choice? Did someone get sick? An accident, fate, a burden? An end.

Surely, they looked around one last time, the way so many families had done before and walked into the sunset, leaving behind their dreams for someone else to sew back together. She had cradled her babies in her arms, the way I do now in her place, standing before that lace adorned window. My Bible sits open as I seek His comfort.

She must have watched, as I do, the cowboys as they bring the last of the remnant and brand the slicks with a brand that will undoubtedly expire. Our expiration date has come ... the one that says we must move on.

The ghosts will be all that remain here when we take the dirt road back to town one last time. They're left to mingle and haunt the bleached bones of crippled horses, old cows, and unfortunate calves.

The market did crash on top of an already bad year. The feed is gone and most of the cows didn't breed back. The owners are cutting their losses while we tear loose of the grasp we had on our future.

So, we'll pack what is left of our hope, and standing in a similar spot on the floor, we'll look around realizing that we are leaving an artifact or two for future consideration by some other family. One who will run horses through the pens again, work cattle down below the window where Mama will cradle the next generation of hopes and dreams in the American West.

Frances Vance

Ridin' Drag

I never minded ridin' drag
You've got the perfect view
Get to see what's up ahead
Laid out in front of you.

On a cow-calf outfit
Specially, trailing pairs
Watch the little new borns
See how well they fare.

New born gets too wobbly?
Ease 'em from the drive
Pair will often drift on in
After the herd arrives.

Cow with leg a draggin'
Come along on her own
Ol' gal there, breathin' hard
Will make it, if left alone.

Young hands don't like the drag
For them, it's just too slow
I just don't understand
That need to blow and go.

If that was the job that day,
Bringin' the pairs all in
Shows the kind of crew we were
Shape of cattle at the pens.

Never minded ridin' drag
Some facts I will avow
You can't move any faster
Than that ol' slowest cow.

Mary Abbott

Watching . . . waiting

Watching the drought deepen from my office window, I see more and more deer and elk sneaking into the water troughs in the early morning and at twilight. The yard and corrals are full of birds, hundreds sometimes, searching for anything to eat and savoring the water that is here. Dust is beginning to blow again, canceling my plans to go ride and see all the new babies—my lungs are still suffering from a bout with the flu. Weather folks claim it is the driest it has been for a hundred and twenty-five years; we've had no real winter, no days of long-johns and wool hats. I join the praying for rain and snow reverberating throughout the Southwest.

Deanna Dickinson McCall

Triangle HC Days

The Harper family went to work for McElhaney Cattle Company, better known as the 7L, which included the old Triangle HC, once a dude ranch. We usually needed to live at Headquarters from May through October, and perhaps part of November.

My husband's cousin had sent her son to work for us one summer. He was about fifteen, same age as our son. His friends called him Chucko. A big, burly lad who seemed to "clunk" through life rather than walk easy.

August always gave us a few days to rest. We homeschooled during slack work periods, and that was scheduled between seven and noon every morning. Then the bunch was turned loose to play. As young ones often do, there was a lot of running inside then back outside, leaving doors open.

I caught one of my daughters as she came through, and sent her to a storeroom in another building for a special piece of material I wanted to measure for a shirt. She flew through the kitchen, the dining room, and on out the back door where she hot-footed up the trail. Coming back with my material under her arm, she was headed for the still-open door. As I walked to the door to accept her burden, I looked down at something moving through the threshold. It was the biggest timber rattler I'd ever seen, slowly crawling into that door just as she was getting ready to step through.

"STOP!" I yelled.

"What?" she retorted.

"Rattler!" was all I could get out. That eight-year-old girl LEAPED past me, hit the floor a yard away, and jumped three feet high to hit the dining room table with both feet, screaming all the way.

I saw the snake slip inside and crawl behind the book case. Seeing Chucko out the front window, I yelled, "Bring that hoe, and come in the back door. QUICK."

As I watched where the rattler was headed, she was doing a

jig up and down on the poor wobbly table. I thought it would surely collapse beneath her.

Chucko came stomping, as I knew he would, carrying the hoe. I snuck quietly over to ease the book case away from the wall so he could see where the rattler was. He clomped over with his hoe, and with all that loud noise, the snake started coiling, its old tongue in and out testing the air.

Chucko eased forward, after finally locating the snake where I was pointing. "Wait, Aunt Roni, I'll go get my .22 off my saddle."

"WHAT? NO! He'll get away. Give me that hoe." I grabbed it, and with a few good, well placed whacks, he was beheaded. I handed Chucko back the hoe and helped the hysterical girl off the table, while Chucko carefully walked outside and threw what was left under the tree outside the back door and buried the head deep in the ground.

Ascencion, a kindly Mexican hired to help give Harp a hand, heard when I yelled to Chucko, and came up from the barn to see what the screeching was all about. He gathered up that snake and took what was left of the rattles.

I was disturbed as I wasn't keen on messing around with dead rattlesnakes. I had seen them strike even after they were dead, so I preferred he leave it be. I asked him, "Why don't you leave snake there? Put mucho terra over." (My husband used to laugh at my meager efforts to communicate in my efforts at their language.)

"No, no, Señora. Dry the meat, ground up, put on . . ." he paused. "*Muy Bueno* for . . ." he motioned scratching an itch.

Well, I'd heard it all. Only weeks before his grandson, who was staying with him for a few weeks, had killed a rattler at the barn and prepared it gourmet style and served it to us for dinner!

Guess you know, after that, those doors were closed very carefully.

Roni Harper

Do I wish?

Do I wish I had tried harder?
Stayed longer?
Given more?
Do I wish I had tried harder?
Dug deeper?
Cried less?
Do I wish I had tried harder?

Sometimes.
When I bury my head in the curve of a shoulder, smell that
one-of-a-kind scent of horse and sweat. When I see baby calves
hit the ground running, bucking and bawling, playing along the
trail while mothers meander.

Sometimes.
When spring hits the earth with her breath of warmth, and the
grass turns green and the hillsides are splattered with color.
When life returns and water runs deep and the cattle are fat.
When shipping trucks bring company, and news from over the
hill.

Never.
When wolves had taken our full calf crop. When we find the
hides of mama cows with bones of babies half born and eaten by
ravens and coyotes. When the drought has maimed the hillsides,
and the land is dry and desolate. When horses are thin, and
stand by the windmill waiting for the wind to turn her blades
enough to fill the tank again.

Do I wish I had tried harder?
Stayed longer?
Given more?
Do I wish I had tried harder?
Dug deeper?
Cried less?
Do I wish I had tried harder?
Sometimes.

Sally Harper Bates

THEY DON'T KNOW

One summer afternoon while I was tending bar at Matt's Saloon in Prescott, a nice lady from the Valley came in and sat at the bar. We got to talking and come to find out she was the one who started "Waste Not, Want Not." A society who goes out and retrieves good food that would normally get thrown out and gets it to hungry needy people. She told me that her favorites were the children.

She told me the next time she came up she would bring me some photos of the little sharecropper's kids and immigrant kids.

It was fall when she showed back up, and like she had promised, she brought the photos, a whole stack of black and whites. As I was going through them I noticed all the little children were clean and had big smiles on their little faces.

When I handed them back to her I said, "For being so poor, they sure are happy!"

Her reply was, "Yes, they are. They don't know they are poor!"

I remember thinking, "No wonder ranch kids are so happy."

Karen Perkins

I CAN'T HEAR THE HOOFBEATS ANY MORE

I can't hear the hoof beats anymore
When I close my eyes and listen
I've been gone too long from the life I love
Where the sounds and smells remind me
That I have a place on earth
Where I was happy and wild and free.
I can't hear the hoof beats anymore
Too long gone and too far away
Reaching back to another day
A time of joy and freedom sweet
A time of happiness pure and complete.
I can't hear the leather creaking
On a saddle that fits me and my horse
I need to hear them when life rushes in
But I can't close my eyes and see them again
They are fading away in the fog of time
Those memories sweet that were all mine
And I can't hear the hoof beats anymore.
My link to that life walked out the door
Taking the keys to that life
No longer a cowboy or partner
No longer a cowboy's wife.
I try so hard to hear them
They are what kept me sane
When I could not be there
To mount and ride again
But time is cruel and slips away
And soon it is up and gone
And I can't hear the hoof beats
Feel the leather and mane
And I know I will never be happy again
For I can't hear the hoof beats anymore.

Janet Moore

HAPPY WIFE, HAPPY LIFE

We're all grateful for the men we've known, families that we have met along the way. For roundup crews and little ones watching from fences. Life in the West requires the treasure of friendships and good neighbors.

Getting ready for the works, I begin to smell the meat and onions brazing in the big ol' black skillet. I throw taters and gravy mixin's together, then add tea by the gallon. Lots of coffee too.

I cook a big breakfast for all the men to eat, clean the kitchen, and quickly grab my gear. I can hear the rigs coming down the bumpy road. Men are loading horses. It's crunch time.

John got my horse saddled, and I quickly finished my chores. I do not want to embarrass hubby by being too girly and too slow.

We haul up to the drop ground, unload, and get our orders. I ride the circle today. I know that pasture, and so does my dog. She is good as gold, sweet as honey, unless a cow decides to cross her. That will "make her day."

We shuffle around the wires, shooing cattle as we go. These are home-grown girls, they know the deal. We'll dump our stuff into the big bunch and work them after dinner. My job here is done for now.

I head on back to the cook house to finish up the meal, make sure I got enough biscuits in the pans to be ready, right on time. It's hot and it's dirty. We need a lot of something cool to drink. But the boys will want coffee, too. We waste no time at this noon break; we'll visit when the work is done.

Headin' back to the working pens, I'm careful not to forget my gloves. I hate to get my hands all trashy. I do my best to make sure I hold up my end of the crew, not whine too much, or get in the way, just be where I am supposed to be so I'll make a hand today.

I love working cattle. Women can do the doctoring, ear mark, tally books, and in a pinch grab that branding iron and proceed to do the artwork. It's dusty and dirty, but oh, such wonderful years in the middle of dust, and dirt, and roundup crews.

Susan Gahr

THE PROPOSAL

I never dreamed of ranching or had thoughts along those lines,
Till I met my darling husband, who was the ranching kind.
He said, "I know you will love the life we'll build out here,
Days are long, the work is hard, but the rewards are very dear.

We'll be providing beef, that's raised here on the range,
And doing something more important, in these times of change.
We'll be raising children, who know what's right from wrong,
Who understand life and death, and fight for weak and strong.

They'll pass along our values, they're sure to fill our shoes.
Please join me in this way of life, there's no way we can lose."
And, when he placed that golden band on my extended hand,
I had to smile, for on that ring, was our cattle brand!

Betty Burlingham

* I was born a "townie" and became a molecular biologist. Ranching was not in my radar, but I wanted children and a family. I'm sure glad I accepted this proposal. It's been 38 wonderful years and three children who are amazing young adults. There is no better place to raise children than a ranch.

WHEN ROADS WERE HARD TO FIND

There was a road there yesterday, until the rain we prayed for came in spades. Oh, we needed that blessed water falling from the sky—needed it badly. But did it have to come all at once?

I'm running low on provisions. It's been two months since I used that road for anything more than a check on the mailbox. We'll have to be satisfied with beans and biscuits tonight, and I realized this morning there are weevils in the bottom of the flour bin. Daniel says, "They don't eat much." I'll clean it out before I put the fresh batch in next week. And it will be next week before we get out of this camp.

The water came down hard, and short of being pulled across by horses, there is no way out. That will have to wait a couple of days for the water to subside; then we'll try it. Daniel won't want to take a chance of having the auto washed down stream.

I'll miss the visit with Emma and Mabel. We planned to meet for coffee at the Old Mill, maybe lunch if there was money left in my pocketbook after groceries. They'll be there waiting for me, but they know it rained. Will they talk about me while I'm gone? Oh, I'm sure of it.

I'll miss the sale at the local J.C.Penny store, and that is truly sad. They have material four yards for a dollar. That would make new shirts for Daniel, and maybe even a new apron for me. The old one is torn where I caught it on the fence post chasing cattle out of the hay stack.

The hay stack. *Oh Lord, how wet is the hay stack?*

Sally Harper Bates   *memories of a friend.*

26

Saying farewell

It is hard to see them struggle when they owe you nothing." Her words jumped out of the text she sent me.

It had not gone the way I had thought. I was hoping just to find him one morning laying in a peaceful forever sleep. Instead, we struggled together for a few days. One of those, not quite as hard as the others, our vet came to see him, and he seemed better for a short time.

It was tough watching him try to stay up on all four feet. I could not effectively describe the relief of having my husband doing the hard part, standing with him keeping him upright until his heart that had kept him going for thirty-three years could not hold him up anymore. Our vet friend stood by us.

It wasn't our first farewell to beloved horses, but he had been with us the longest. Very few enjoy the privilege of realizing the truth about the animal God created when horses were on His mind.

We got him as a three-year-old stud. He had been fed in a trailer to get him from California to Arizona, his destiny carried in the hands of my sister. She gave him to my husband, so he became a part of my family.

Like many family horses, he carried us all through years of life. Cowboying, rodeoing, life changing events of illness, death, injuries, weddings, babies, moving, defeat, success, high school, college, work, no work. He watched as others came and went, but he always had first place at the feed trough.

On that unforgettable evening, we stroked his shiny coat and rubbed his ole wise eyes, and told him to rest because try as he might he was not able to stand. I walked away as he laid his head back after the final attempt to stand was a failure. I could not watch him struggle a moment longer. The coward in me overcame the spirit of courage. Though God gave me a spirit of power and love I could not dig deeper to watch my friend breathe his last.

Our farewell story is like those of many horse lovers. Friendship with a horse is unique. They race their way into our lives and take over in bits and pieces in so many ways. Having the kind of love for them I do, I will always stop and stare when I see some special one. I will strain to my toes, and put a kink in my neck to get a better look at them. If they are moving too fast my mind will drink in the slightest opportunity to visit the image of them again. I will never see one that it doesn't reach into my soul and rest somewhere in the deeper crevices.   mr. Leo Rass / garie

More eloquent writers have spoken better than I am able about these awesome creatures, but I was called to a deeper understanding of the profound truth of my friend's words, "When they owe you nothing."

The book of Job 38:19-25 reads, "Do you give the horse his strength or clothe his neck with a flowing mane? Do you make him leap like a locust, striking terror with his proud snorting? He paws fiercely, rejoicing in his strength, and charges into the fray. He laughs at fear, afraid of nothing; he does not shy away from the sword, the quiver rattles against his side, along with the flashing spear and lance. In frenzied excitement he eats up the ground; he cannot stand still when the trumpet sounds: At the blast of the trumpet he snorts, 'aha.' He catches the scent of battle from afar, the shout of commanders and the battle cry."

Thank you old friend, you taught us well.

Even in your final moments of selfless giving.

Perilee Sharp

WHO DROPPED THE CAKE?

We were on our way to the neighbors for dinner, and I was assigned to dessert duty, so I baked a big chocolate cake. When I reached in to take it out of the oven, the pot holder was so thin I burned my fingers, and of course, the cake went upside down right in the middle of the kitchen floor.

No time to bake another, so I scooped it up and stood waiting for some kind of lightbulb to go on with an idea.

I remembered seeing a dessert in some magazine where they cut up pieces of cake and put jam on it with whipped cream. We had plenty of fresh cream from the milk cow, so I whipped it up and built my own version.

Rescuing pieces of cake, I cut them into small squares, layered them in a bowl with strawberry jam and whipped cream, and presto! It was lovely . . . if I do say so myself!

When I arrived, dessert in hand, all smiles, the neighbor said, "Oh, you must have got the recipe from Emma—she brought that to the Cowbell's meeting last week!"

My son looked up innocently and said, "Did she drop her cake on the floor too?"

Sequent Bodine

The gift

The leaves crumble beneath my horse's hooves, scattering into flakes onto the gray rock as we climb up the trail. We've labored up this trail, hoof striking rock to dust repeatedly, through oak brush that never turned green, algarita too dry to produce the berries I cherish for jelly, and rust colored cedar and pinon stands. The stunted grass lies buried in dust.

We are riding to the high country today, hoping enough rain fell at this elevation to make a little grass, enough grass to hold over at least some cows. Signs of feral hogs appear; they've rooted up prickly pear and made divots under the trees. We're surprised to see how high they've traveled; elevations like this are not common hog environment. So many animals are displaced with this phenomenal drought, all seeking food and precious water.

We stop the horses, letting them catch their breath. I view the river bottom far below, winding through the serpentine canyon. The river bed is gray rock; reminiscent of the dead rattlesnakes turned on their backs in belief the gesture will bring rain. Nothing remains to show it was once a life-giving stream. I am gifted with the remembrance of the music of the water, the graceful green willows, elms, and cottonwoods that used to flourish there. I also recall this mountain, knee deep in dew-laden gramma, blue stem, and side oats, swaying with wildflowers in a gentle breeze. Calves and their mothers, sleek and fat, frolicked up and down the mountainsides.

We turn the horses and continue our journey in search of feed. Study the hillsides, seeing stands of grass in protected areas, under the trees, beside boulders and brush. Brown, dry grass, but feed for the cows we're trying to hang on to. The farther we climb the thicker the grass becomes. The rocks and altitude enabled this country to hang on to the moisture long enough to let something grow.

Water is the next issue; the spring went dry a year ago. The nine miles of pipeline strung across the mountains and canyons feeding dirt ponds and fiberglass tanks are useless. Running the dozer up the trail will be the next chore, making a crude road so water can be hauled for the cattle we will push up here to winter.

We tie our horses to a tree limb and pull out the lunch we've carried in the saddle bags. I settle on the ground, with a rock for back support, while the horses tear the dry grass into mouthfuls they can eat around their bits. The only clean area on the saddle is where I sat; the rest is covered in the grayish red dust of the mountains. The dust that leaves grit on my skin, in my clothes, and in my house. Even here, moving a boot raises the eternal dust.

Back at the ranch, I pull my dusty saddle off the horse whose sweat is dried and stiff, to find brown leaves and needles that had worked their way under the blankets from the brush we'd gone through. I know I will find the same in my clothing later. I watch the horses munch on the hay, wondering if they've lost track, like I have, of their last bite of green grass.

The cows in the next pen mill around, hoping I'm bringing hay to them. These cattle know me; I've fed cake to them for months in the mountains, some coming close enough to take a cube from my hand. They recognize my face, and my stance, and call to me. I've had to fend some off at times, big Brangus cows pushing and shoving to get to me and the feed sacks I carry on my hip as I scatter the feed on the ground. They've been brought home so we can cull them, again. I am tired of having to choose which cows will stay and which will go. I wonder if this drought will dictate when it is our turn to not make the cut, and we will have to leave the ranch.

I finish throwing hay and scooping grain, watching the birds surrounding the water troughs as I walk towards the house. I start the water in the garden, wading through rows of vegetables in knee high boots and spurs, chasing out a hen who craves the green as well.

We've been through droughts, some short, some lasting years. The current drought is too severe, too long, reported to be drier than the infamous Dust Bowl years. This drought has a death-hold.

Deer come into our corrals, no longer fearing the horses and cattle that used to hold them at bay. A chip downloaded from the game camera placed above the trough displays fox, coyote, javelina, raccoons and other creatures, a far wider range of wild-life than we had believed were coming in. The bear and lions lumbering up were an indisputable fact of desperation.

We will be horseback in the morning, studying cows and bulls, making up yet another load for the sale. The cow whose calf disappeared, the big eared one whose calf didn't grow out, but "burned up" are first choices. Big Tits, who we kept the last couple of years despite her appearance since she grew such good calves until this year, will go. There will be others, and bulls no longer needed for the reduced herd size. The dust will hang in the early light, a haze over the corrals we ride through with grim lined faces and eyes tearing.

Yet, we have a gift. We must have above average memories, to remember where things are in a vast land, which cow hangs with what group, what canyon runs into a main one, and where water may be found. It is this memory that sustains us, memories of green grass, creeks spilling over, cattle rolling in their fat, shiny hides. Memories of what was and what we pray will come again.

Deanna Dickinson McCall

A COWGIRL'S QUEST

We had been searching for our new bull
The weather turned hot, we tried to stay cool
We looked on the mountains and below
Every place that a bull might want to go.

Heading off to church one Sunday morn
Especially proud of the dress I'd worn
Driving east on Highway 93
I spotted another place he could be.

I quickly pulled off to the road side
Got out of the car and swallowed my pride
Hiking my skirts as the cars whirled by
I crossed the rail as fast as I could fly.

From rock to rock I leapt with great care
For the sandals I wore left my toes bare
Seeing there were no cattle around,
I started back over uneven ground.

I waited for a lull in traffic,
Hoping to be discreet and less graphic
I pictured myself, with skirts up high
Straddling the guardrail as cars drove by

What a sight I must have presented!
Some may have thought me to be demented.
No passer by would ever have guessed,
That strange scene was a cowgirl on a quest.

Lola Chiantaretto

Hooves and horns

In the 1930's, Evelyn Perkins sent many letters to the Arizona Cattlegrower's publication, Hooves and Horns. *Here are a few excerpts from those offerings.*

August 1939 ~ August in Arizona, and mud on the floors! Boasting? Well, yes. But it seems so grand to have rain again that I can't help but boast. Who cares about the mud tracked in? The grass will grow and cows will eat.

July 1934 ~ Some day, when cattle prices go up so that it won't take a whole herd to do this, I am going to buy a copy of every western magazine and then tell you my honest opinion of each!

February 1936 ~ I used to smile when people told of old Daniel Boone saying the country was getting too closely settled; he'd have to move when someone moved within twenty-five miles of him. Now I know how he felt. When I first moved to Perkinsville, Prescott was forty-five miles away with the road not much more than a trail. Williams was only about thirty miles as the crow flies, but almost a hundred by road. Jerome was about eighty. But now, with all the new roads on the ranch, Jerome is only eighteen, Williams thirty-four, and Prescott forty-five over a fine country dirt road. We have a WPA Camp here in our pasture, and they have picture shows on Friday nights. All of this is fine, but it doesn't feel like a ranch any more! Like Daniel Boone, I'm getting too civilized.

July 1935 ~ Up near Williams lives a little known poet, Edna Cole. When man-created things begin to get on my nerves, I love to hop in the car, cross the Verde River and go up, and up, out of the cedars into the great pine country near Williams. I can't describe the region, with its extinct volcanoes marked with red cinders, now splotched with great ferns. Crimson cactus blooms gleaming against gray rocks, and the many-colored Sycamore Canyon. And everywhere those towering pines. It does give the most marvelous cure for the ills of indoors. I know of nothing like it. If I can't get that far away, Indian ruins are close and I love to prowl over them. Some of the arrowheads are so beautifully made they are almost like jewels. So small, usually not two inches long. Then, too, one finds many tiny shards of pottery. This was once the crossroads of many tribes they say. According to the Denver University, one small box of shards contained as many varieties as the famous Heinz 57 varieties!

1935 ~ I've sometimes had trouble getting somebody to mail my letters, but my oldest, Marion, eleven years old, haunts the post office since he mailed his order for a pair of boots to the Nocona Boot Company. So now, it's no trouble at all to get him to go! I kind of hate to know the boots will be here soon. Oh, I wonder if Ben doesn't need a pair?

August 1937 ~ Our July rains have started and aren't they glorious? They say New England in October can't be equaled for its colors, but you might spare a glance at old Bill Williams Mountain when the aspen leaves turn yellow and make fields of gold on the mountainside among the deep green of the evergreens. The rocks and ground supply any additional colors your heart might crave if you tire, as I never do, of the glowing gold and green. WOW! Hear that thunder? Here comes another rain. Isn't it grand living in Arizona?

Letters by Evelyn Perkins
Supplied by Karen Perkins

TAPESTRY OF KNOTS

In the quiet-time of morning,
when the moon is going down,
She builds a cook-stove fire
with yester-news from town.
And, as warmth creeps into the cabin,
measured slowly by degrees,
She sits with pen at kitchen table
with a quilt to warm her knees.

And she writes of thoughts she garnered
during chores of day before
While she pitched the hay from feed sled
which she prayed would travel slower.
Upon her pad of yellow paper,
dormant words will come to life,
As her mind creeps far from mundane walls,
before she became a rancher's wife.

She can travel (at the speed of ink)
to those places in the heart:
When romance bloomed like summer's rose
or a dream broke and fell apart.
She still can see, with clarity,
a dozen years gone past,
When love was new or love was cold
or a spirit had been slashed.

With open, honest invitation
to explore her hidden thoughts,
She scribes haunting, hunted images
like a tapestry of knots.
And she types them up on linen paper
so they'll be worthy to be read.
Then, she dons her crusted coveralls
for there are cattle to be fed.

How many more are like her?
we can only guess.
Those women who write heart-broke words,
emboldened to confess.
They fold, they stamp, and they mail
their souls from coast to coast
And share their work with all the world
except the one they love the most.

Virginia Bennett

KELLY VIRGINIA

A family had a job to do, it didn't matter she was young
By the shade of a mesquite bush she'd play till they were done
She grew up in Arizona, on the Slaughter's Ranch
Not afraid of a hard day's work, she learned to hunt and brand

With her yellow hair in a ponytail like the yellow horse she rides
Sitting tall in the saddle, Dad and Grandad by her side
Gatherin' cattle or huntin' lions, she worked more than she played
She spent some time in Houston, but Arizona is where she stayed

She's a huntress, a cowgirl like no other
A wife and a mother, as steady as the mule she rides
Strong as a thorn, soft as a rose
Living out the life she chose
She's a ray of sunshine at first light
She's a star in the night

Now her little girl is five years old with the same yellow hair
Born with a rope in her hands, living life without a care
Side by side with her mom she'll ride, dawn to setting sun
But you won't hear them complain, there is work to be done

Kip Calahan Young

KIDS

Spring coming meant riding farther from the house to make the Burro Creek "gather." We were waiting for our Calvert course books to come for the three young girls to continue their years of home schooling. Harper needed all of us to clean out close to the O RO fence which joined McElhaney's line on the west side of Burro Creek.

This meant a long ride from Lovelace Cabin up the trail to a small dam where we would cross over and continue through extremely rugged country. "Wait a minute" bushes, mountain laurel, and oak brush were thick.

Cattle had trailed over to the O RO fence, and with binoculars we could see a few cows, calves, and at least two bulls on the other side of the canyon.

Harper sent Chuck over a narrow dam to start those animals towards the Lovelace place. The outfit had been lucky to get a couple of inches of rain and the aphelaria was really heavy around the Mesa.

Harp led out the trail on the side, with me and our oldest daughter, Jimi. Next two, Peri and Jeanie, were to get high enough to head off, turn back and pick up cattle higher up that might try to slip away through the brush.

We scattered. High up on the ridge Harp motioned Jimi to go back and try to hold the cows Chuck would start across the dam. He was waiting with several head in check he wanted to send her way. Harp was four or five hundred feet up the trail. Both were positioned where they could see what was unfolding.

She turned back on her little half-Welsh pony, and of course that little mount did not want to leave the other horses. She had to use her spurs. She urged him, and he jumped forward, losing his balance, and his right foreleg and a back leg started slipping down an embankment.

All I could see from my vantage point was her and her mount disappearing over the edge in a cloud of dust and rocks boiling down. I saw Chuck spur his horse across the dam and saw Harp way up the trail looking back.

I knew I couldn't reach her fast; all I could do was what I'd learned to do when we moved to that rock pile of a ranch. Pray.

By the time the dust settled and my heart stopped beating six hundred miles an hour, man and beast were back on the trail. We finished the job and were riding back to the house when I finally couraged up enough to ask her if she was okay.

"Sure. I was a little scared at first, but mostly I was mad at this horse." She swung her reins against his shoulder and pushed him into a trot. She made it to the corrals ahead of the rest of us.

Roni Harper

ON TRACK

Be it a wedding, job interview, funeral, or party
    this was part of the routine.

Probably more importantly
    it makes a person feel like a king or a queen.

It was with me on my honeymoon,
    and stayed with me all my life.

If you asked my husband he'd say
    it's one of the things that make me a good wife.

If I, or someone I love, needed a boost to get a foot up,
    this was the thing I would give them for luck.

It's something that requires a tad bit of time,
    the rewards in return are simply sublime.

It nothing secret, I will tell you right now.
    your grandmas did it and I'll tell you how.

You start with the collar, the yokes, and the sleeves.
    work side- back- side you'll complete it with ease.

When you or the person you love slips it on your back.
    Ahhh . . . a freshly ironed shirt . . . my life is on track!

Jody Drake

Wash Day, 1921

I remember Mary's visit as if it were yesterday. We look out the alley gate to see her coming, holding a bag of wood for the fire she will build. She hitched a ride from the reservation on a horse-drawn wagon filled with wood for sale. She smiles and hugs two little girls waiting for the day they so love to begin.

Before any work, Mother invites Mary into the kitchen for coffee and conversation, a short one, each woman speaking only a few words of their common language, Spanish.

Then Mary builds a small fire in an area enclosed with bricks. On it she sets the wash tub then drops cut-up brown soap into the boiling water. I take the broom handle and stir and stir then let my little sister take a turn at this important task. On a wooden bench beneath the cottonwoods, Mary sets the rinse water and the bluing water, her secrets to white-as-snow sheets and towels.

Often Mary brings a grandchild or two, some bearing names from my mother's large family. Sometimes Mary's cousin Chona comes too, never doing a lick of work, just sitting with her full skirt spread out on the cement walkway, smoking Bull Durham and eating Mary's food.

When the clothes and linens are dry, folded, put away, Mary's work day is over. I join my parents on the drive to the reservation, a tiny oasis in the middle of the desert south of town.

One stop on the way allows Mary to spend her dollar at the grocery store. I wave good-bye to Mary, already anxious for the next wash day.

For my wedding, Mary gave me a basket
woven with yucca and devil's claw.
Now I am passing this cherished present to you
and with it this story of Mary's enduring gifts.

Janet McMillan Rives As told to me by my mother, Louise Littlefield McMillan (1915-2006)

A MIRACLE

We learned to ride broncy horses 'cause we refused to walk home
And before we were teens we went out on big circles, alone
We started packing pocket knives as soon as we turned five
And even before that we were learning how to drive.

We were turned loose with ropes, bows, and BB guns
Where the snakes rattle and fast creeks run
We played tag in pastures with ornery mama cows
And had no fear of crossing streets or wandering off in town.

We followed our dads on trap lines and ran some of our own
Raced around on barebacked horses with no emergency phone
We halter broke 4-H steers, got kicked and drug for fun
And as soon as we sold the suckers, we went out and bought a gun.

We hated horsemanship helmets,
Didn't even know they made 'em for bikes
Were learning how to run four-wheelers
While our peers were still on trikes

We rode wagons down steep hills solely for the crash
Every single game we played, revolved around contact
We climbed trees about to blow over, trying to build forts,
And tried to build rafts out of rotted barn wood boards.

We played in old outbuildings falling down around our ears
And our battle scars just kept getting bigger through the years
It's a good thing we had our Mamma's prayers
    and the Good Lord on our side.
'Cause it's nothing short of a miracle that we all survived

We told each other "you're not THAT hurt" oh so many times.
It really is a miracle that we all survived.

Randi Johnson

MY DESERT HOME

I step out in the morning
Cup of coffee in my hand
Sun peeks over the mountain
Sunlight creeps across the land

It crawls across the mountains
Leaping canyons and the draws
Highlights the mountain peaks
I watch it all in awe.

Then as the sun climbs higher
The soft light settles on the trees
Mesquites all clothed in yellow blossoms
Their branches sway gently in the breeze

And then the great saguaros are
Shining in the light
White crowns upon their tops
The guardians of the night

I sit back in my chair and listen
I hear the cactus wren and quail
A dove is softly calling as
A hawk above us sails

I long for the monsoon rains
The thunder and the lightning
They can appear so quickly
With a rage that's almost frightening

Then the raindrops hang like diamonds
On the Palo Verde trees
The sweet scent of wet greasewoods
Floats lightly on the breeze

The desert dust is in my veins
Nowhere else can compare
Can't think of any other place
I'd rather be than here.

Suzi Killman

Tater Donuts

Double O Ranch Seligman, Arizona, 1985

I was cooking during Fall works. Yates Dixon was about seven years old, workin' with his dad, Chip, and the cowboy crew. Yates would take some of the short rides, but stayed in camp on long days.

Every day he'd throw diesel on the fire, I mean he made an inferno and really get'er hummin'. Then he would find me to inquire: "Is it time to make the donuts yet?"

We fried 'em every day, used lots of Crisco. Everyone sure enjoyed the donuts, and Yates became the donut expert that fall.

Recipe: "Tater Donuts for Yates"

3 tsp oil or Crisco melted
¾ c sugar
2 eggs
1 cup mashed potatoes
¼ cup milk
1 ½ cups flour
3 tsp baking powder
1 tsp salt
½ tsp nutmeg (If you have it)
About 1-1½ inches from can of Crisco for deep frying (add if needed) Uses lots of Crisco, but it's worth it.
1 large cast iron skillet or Dutch oven

Cream shortening and add sugar. Mix thoroughly, add eggs, then potatoes and milk. Blend well. Mix dry ingredients together; add milk to mixture until a soft dough. Additional flour may be added to make easier handling. Roll out about 1/2" thick, cut out donuts and fry in deep fat. Makes about 30.

Sandy Heller

LOFT OF DREAMS

I climb the shaft of splintered beams
Into the loft of broken dreams
Where scattered in the hay and dust
Abandoned plans are turned to rust.

So silent and so still they seem
As though they'd never been.
But I remember birthing these
And giving life to them.

What now are boxes bound in twine
And set aside to store,
Once were sacred dreams of mine
That have a life no more.

Oh, but I remember years
I had these in our home.
There's my battered sewing shears
And those curtains I had sewn.

There's the harness for our team
That pulled our wagon load
Of supplement and fence wire ream
Down a rocky, rutted road.

I see old branding irons we used
On new calves in the spring.
And weathered saddle parts refused
By cowboys for their string.

I find the milk strainer is stacked
On a ledge against the wall
It saw its share of use back when
Three children were yet small.

So many things make me fly
To a life that's now surreal
Of when family, earth and sky
Were my soul's substantial meal.

Here scattered memories are strewn
Like random stars at night.
Emotions rise from depths unknown
I've worked to hide from sight.

I realize they've been stored away
Like items on the shelf.
Forgotten, but not gone to stay. . .
Buried within myself.

Why are notes of my life-span
Now packed and stashed to store?
Were they but parcels of a plan
That matter now no more?

I hear the words "Not true" ring clear
And echo through the air.
"From what you've conjured up so dear,
I've brought forth jewels most rare."

I know the stars are not by chance
Placed in the midnight sky.
Nor was my setting "happenstance"
That seems a dream gone by.

What I see now as boxes bound
Is treasured beauty stored.
In memories and visions found
That cannot be ignored.

My loft of dreams transcends
The limitations that I've known
Of time and space that do not end . . .
A place that I called home.

The quintessence of the life I've known
Is now a vision grand.
Where cattle grazed and cowboys roamed
Off in a distant land.

Shawn Cameron

Pincurls & leggins

It was a bitter cold morning when I threw my saddle on my horse, headed for a day ride with what was to be partly a pincurl crew, (an old name for one that included girls).

Ulla came by to get me, we loaded my horse into the trailer with hers, while our breath hung frozen in the air.

I had layers of stuff on: long johns, three undershirts, wooly shirt, jacket, wild rag, high top boots, wool socks, jeans and chinks. When you're livin' on ranch wages you better learn how to be real thrifty. I bought whatever my family needed wherever I could find it . . . for a good price. I found me some long johns, straight from the Norwegian army. I knew they had to be good! Most of my wooly wardrobe came from the Salvation Army in Prescott.

I kid you not, we were near froze stiff when we started. But the country side was breathtaking, both in its beauty and the cold. Trees looked like they were cut from fine crystal glass, ice everywhere.

We drove on to the drop, mounted our ponies, and headed for the breaks. We enjoyed ourselves, in spite of the cold, visiting as we trotted out.

It wasn't long we had us a pretty good little bunch gathered, and it kept growing, as did the temperature.

Mid-winter in Yavapai County, Arizona, the sun was heating things up rapidly, and before long I was sweating gumdrops.

I waved Ulla to a stop.

"I mean, I am . . . so hot. I got to strip some of these layers off." I found a little growth of brush, which was a miracle in itself. There was little-to-no cover in all directions. Ulla stood guard, and the cows didn't mind the stop.

I got myself kind of hid away. If you've ever "been there," you know you can't slip anything off when it is soaking wet! I was all stuck together like glue, ITCHING EVERYWHERE! Could hardly get my chinks off, never mind the boots, or wet wool socks. I stripped down and got my woolies off, hung everything on limbs, then started the process to redress.

Of course, you guessed it; that's when we heard cows bawling and squalling from all directions! Cows and cowboys crawling everywhere.

I hurried as fast as I could, Ulla giving me the high sign to hurry up. I got myself put back together, rolled up my woolies and tied them on the back of my saddle. We proceeded to the hold up ground.

The grub wagon was pulling in, so we took the noon break. Some hobbled their horses, but I just kept mine with me, tied off to a nearby tree.

It was quiet, everybody was hungry, focused on getting a plate full of good grub. Got rested. The boss got up, time to go back to work.

I stepped on my horse and heard one of the men ride by and chuckle. "Hey, Suzie, are them your undies tied on the back of your saddle?"

Susan Gahr

Daughter of the Desert

She runs with scissors and plays with matches,
    her mom calls her "Wind in Her Face,"
She's feathers, and flowers, and grass in her hair,
    denim, and leather, and lace,
She is the desert wind,
    she is a wild rose,
She dances in the sage,
    and sings with the coyotes,
Her tears run the river,
    her laughter rides the breeze,
She is a daughter of the desert, a lady runnin' free.
She laughs, and sings, and dances,
    to some silent, ancient song,
She rides, and ropes, and chases her hopes,
    all the day long,
She runs with scissors, plays with matches,
    dances on the breeze,
She's a daughter of the desert,
    a rose growin' wild and free.

Randi Johnson

AND THEN CAME THE WIND

The sun beat on my face through the dirty window pane. Clouds that bring the rain had become a whispered hope, and I wondered if I dared pray again today. I was afraid that mention of the word out loud would jinx its arrival.

Months had come and gone, and nary even the slightest scent of moisture blew in with the late summer breezes. Drought. Horrid word, horrid thought, horrid impact on the earth and all its inhabitants. Yet it had become a part of us, worse than ever I'd seen it.

The ground groaned, cried out for need of anything wet. Plants were dry, brittle, so stiff not even the wind could coax them to move. Walking through the grass, I could almost hear it crying. Trees were brown, many bare, even evergreens were dying back.

Animals, both wild and domesticated, hung near windmills and springs that were still dripping water. The wild things hovered near, the need for water overriding fear of man.

At long last, for two days it fell. For hours it came slow and steady, and we could almost hear the ground sucking it in. Then it would shift gears, and for another several hours it would pour, run off the surface, and water tanks began to fill. We rejoiced. Even danced in the front yard as it fell and settled.

Then came the wind. With the morning of the third day it blew the clouds over the distant mountains, scattered them across the sky like frightened quail. And it blew . . . hard . . . and it blew for three days as though it meant to tear the siding off the buildings in the meadow.

And it dried out the moisture, sucked up the pools in the tank, drew it out of the leaves and up from the roots until the drought took over again.

I hated the wind that month. Until it decided to blow in another storm, and leave it with us for several days.

I'm fickle that way. I love it when it brings me gifts, hate it when it takes them back.

Sally Harper Bates

WHEN THE TIME COMES TO LEAVE

For numerous reasons, the time came to move on, to leave the home place. Once the uneasy decision was made, the sale was finalized, and we knew where we were going from here, I rather naively thought the hardest part, psychologically, was behind.

But then with the sorting and packing, came other unsettling events. Decisions had to be made as to what would go and what would of necessity be sold, given away, or left behind. At that point, it became clear how many memories were tied up in these "things" accumulated through the years. Sometimes the letting go was made more difficult for me, because of the connection to people and times that were no more.

On the last day in that old house, empty rooms echoed as I walked across worn wooded floors, made smooth and a lighter shade by so many thousands of footsteps.

One last time, I peered out through the kitchen window that always whistled when the wind blew. Remembered the seemingly endless armloads of firewood we packed in to the stove. Marveling how it somehow managed to keep us warm even in the coldest part of a northwestern winter.

I thought back to all the fences we built, the pastures we irrigated, the cattle we'd run, the good horses we'd ridden, the not-so-good horses we'd ridden, and some we were lucky to get ridden.

Our years there were good, and so are the memories I've kept . . . even as I left behind a little piece of my heart.

Carole Jarvis

Strong Family Branch

I watched my girls together under a hot summer sun,
My eldest and youngest whose lives are far apart
One is married now with kids of her own.
The other is young and wild and full of fun.
They are so much alike in their different worlds.
The four blue-green eyes are thoughtful now
They are both thinking of young men far away.
One brushes her hair back, the other twists a curl.
The same lonely feelings creep over them somehow
Although in age and maturity there is a big gap
the feelings for their loved ones are deeply shared.
One is a busy Navy wife, the other has school and an FFA cow.
The older ponders war, submarines and the pounding sea,
The younger worries about wild cattle and rough horses.
One husband is away fighting for God and country,
While the youth reaps what it's like to be free.
My daughters, I have come to realize
Love deeply the young men they have chosen with pride
In a few years, my youngest will be ready to marry
And it must be a cowboy for this turn of the page.
To a cowboy, and a sailor, the girls' hearts they have hurled
Both men live by a code that is honest and true
They love God, country and family above all else
These are traits hard to find in today's changing world.
I watch my girls so different and yet so alike
One prefers to sit on a rock by the beach
And listen to sea gulls as the waves pound the shore.
She likes picnics and movies and a tandem bike.
Born to be wild is the youngest one's course,
Gather cattle, rope calves, run barrels, and brand.
She will dance with her cowboy till the band stops.
She is beauty and grace on the back of a horse.

Different days. Different ones of my children I ponder,
Today it's these two who make me stop and wonder
About how much their differences make them alike
One still lives at home and the other out yonder.
It seems the values they learned growing up on the ranch
Will, and have, served them well wherever they go.
There will always be a closeness between them.
Whatever the distance, they share a strong family branch.

Charlotte Allgood McCoy

NO BETTER LIFE

The old faucet drips, as slowly she sips
Her coffee in morning's dull glow.
Storm's ragin' a battle, she's home with the cattle.
The temperature reads five below.

Wind was a blowin', it was still snowin',
She stepped out to do morning chores.
The snow was a driftin', with icy snakes siftin',
A solid sheen sealed the barn doors.

Wet flakes stung her face, she steadied her pace;
Her scarf danced an icy staccato.
Wires thrummed out a wail, trees bent to the gale,
Barn eaves moaned a mournful vibrato.

Inside it was still, she forked them their fill
They nickered from stalls safe and warm.
She calmed down their fears, scratched soft neck and ears,
Then plunged right back into the storm.

The truck started rough, but it was enough.
She'd loaded the bales night before.
Then drove from the haystack, with two dogs in the back
And one settled down on the floor.

A drift to the knee, she broke the gate free,
Plowed into the sheltered corral.
With no cows in there yet, but a fella could bet
That horned rip would soon be her pal.

Was it worth the chance, to play the gate dance
In case the old Jessies came in?
She rolled bales to the ground, and glanced round at the sound
Of Horn just a sporting a grin.

Horn sallied right up, and started to sup
On a bale that she'd jerked to the ground.
Ignoring that cow the wife furrowed her brow,
Spread hay with a vigor newfound.

Confronting the cow, she knew that somehow
She'd wrestle that bale on again.
With a wave and a yell, Old Horn could just tell
It was time to move on in the pen.

Now with the cow gone, she tossed the bale on,
The dogs hunkered down by the spare.
She crawled back in the truck, and spun out through the muck,
Back into the rime-frosted air.

Her cowboy's away, thoughts with her today,
He worries for her with the chores.
They warned of the squall, it arrived at nightfall.
He wished she could just stay indoors.

Back home in the gale, she knows without fail
The ice on the tank will be frozen.
A lick of the ax, and several hard whacks;
She thinks of the life that they've chosen.

Shards flew here and there, spray froze in the air.
Ice chunks were soon scattered about.
Cows filtered in slow, and they all seemed to know
She'd be there for them there's no doubt.

Cows walked to their hay, a bovine buffet.
She's glad they'd come in from the range.
Now two years in a drought, but they'd never sell out.
She knew others might think it strange.

Stood watching them eat, the wild wind beat
At her clothes caked and frozen with snow.
Then after awhile, walked off with a smile,
Thought ... no better life she could know.

Valerie Beard

WHEN SADIE MADE A HAND

"Just an old dog." Some would say. Well, I beg to differ.
She was more than just an old dog, Sadie is famous ya' know.
At least to those that knew her, and loved her to the bone.
A natural to cow work, she made it look easy, and made me
 look good.
She never quit. She never cowered. If she got challenged,
Katie bar the door! She more than earned her keep!
As some would say, Sadie "worked like a dog."
Her happiest days were spent working cows. Sadie had no quit;
 she knew how to read 'em and gave 'em what was their due.
She'd let 'em know who was boss, too!
She went to working cows her second year.
She came along the first year, but I kept her close to me.
The second year, she just put herself in the right place at the right
time, and started pushing cows in the right direction.
She knew the pasture, I was astonished. I just let her work.
We'd ride ahead, start them cows to the bunch,
 Sadie would keep 'em moving toward the fence.
When they all got there, she'd push them down the line
 heading toward the gate.
The hillside looked to be crawling with cows.
 Sadie kept them moving all in the right direction and did not
 lose a-one!
She'd have them bunched at the gate before lunch. We'd meet her,
 just in time for a scratch. Sadie with her dog-face smile.
She knew she did good and held her cow batch.
We'd open the gate an' give 'em the boot.
The horses would shuffle along in the sand.
 Ya' know . . . cow work was easy, when Sadie made a hand.

Susan Gahr

FROM MY KITCHEN WINDOW

From my kitchen window I see
The wind rustle through the trees
A rusty old pickup truck
The colts that play and buck

From my kitchen window I see
My children running wild and free
No concern of the time
Nor of the clothes upon the line

From my kitchen window I see
Open country so precious to me
An early hint of coming spring
The geldings in the remuda string

From my kitchen window I see
The dust of the herd on the breeze
The riders who bring up the drag
The little calves who lag

From my kitchen window I see
Cowboys with hearts wild and free
Roans and bays and grays
Shorthorn, Angus and Charlois

From my kitchen window I see
I am exactly where I should be

Mary Matli

WOMEN OF THE WEST

Scared, alone they came to the West
In carriages, wagons, and carts.
Traveling alone, without husbands,
Many people labeled them "tarts."

Most were wholesome, some were shady,
Some bandits, packin' a gun.
Some packin' crates full of school books,
Round glasses, hair up in a bun.

They came from all over the globe.
Their dream was to start a new life.
Women with want ads clutched tightly
Soon to be a stranger's new wife.

These women were white, they were black,
Some skins of brown, yellow, or red.
Raisin' kids in a minin' camp
Or makin' a go on a homestead.

Others sat straddle tall horses
Behind sulky, rangy-boned steers.
From the "good women" in small towns,
Came the mocking glances and sneers.

Others half black or part Indian,
Just hoped to survive in the West.
Because "mixed blood" or of their race,
Had no station among the rest.

All colors worked in the brothels
And saloons found along the way.
Called harlots, they were just women,
Hopeful of a much better day.

From the East, the schoolmarm had come,
Educated, poised and proper.
Determined, she yearned to go West,
Though some tried, no one could stop her.

Slant eyes, with round yellow faces,
Quiet and respectfully shy,
Asian born and bought for labor,
Though young, many often would die.

A few women challenged the norms,
Dressed like men, were quick on the draw.
A crim'nal's life there in the West,
A part of hist'ry, an outlaw.

The ranch wife rode long hours each day
With her husband and weary crew.
Unassisted, she'd unsaddle,
Then cooked up her biscuits and stew.

There were those who buried their young,
Leavin' them on the open plain.
Makeshift markers at tiny graves,
Were soon gone from the wind and rain.

Men alone didn't open the West,
But, women in lace or in suede.
In a time when women were women,
They came west; they settled; they
stayed!

These Were The Women of the West!

Sam DeLeeuw

SPECIAL DELIVERY

We were expecting a baby in the winter of '85.
We had purchased two bulls in November
Not knowing when they would arrive.
It was the eve of the Valentine's holiday,
Hubby said, "Let's go out and play,
Go eat, take in a movie, this baby is due any day."
So we took our three year old to the sitter,
Went out and had a grand time,
Got home a few minutes past midnight
And into the bed so divine.

Awakened by a phone call, Hubby said,
"Get up, get dressed, be bright,
We're meeting the driver in Falkland,
We're having bull delivery tonight."
As I got out of bed, I was met with another surprise
A gush of warm, wet water
Was making its way down my thighs.
I said, "Honey, I think we're delivering
More than bulls tonight."
He said, "OK, get dressed, I love you,
Everything will turn out right."

So, we met the driver in Falkland,
Took our bulls to the very back,
Unloaded his into the corral
For water and a snack,
Made coffee for the driver,
Reloaded, and sent him on his way.
Hubby said, "Well, you're not in labor yet,
So let's just hit the hay."
Just as I was settling in, he said,
"Oh, there is one more need,
Before you can go to the hospital,
We must grind two loads of feed."

We got up bright and early
The grinder pounded grain,
And just as we were finishing,
It began to rain.
Hubby turned to me and he said,
"You look like such a mess!
I suppose you'd like to take some time
To clean up and to rest.
I'm going to work at the Med School,
I'll be back at ten,
Then we can go to the hospital,
And real labor can begin."

So, Valentine's Day was spent
With labor pains and breathing right.
Our baby daughter, Rose Marie,
Was born at fifteen past midnight.
There's a message in this story,
I'd like to share right now,
It takes one tough, strong woman,
To love a doctor who loves his cows!

Betty Burlingham

*Every woman who has delivered a baby has a story about what her partner did or didn't do to help her get that precious child delivered. This is mine, and it is entirely true.

LEARNING TO WALK AGAIN

Knelt by his bed
I cried, my heart bled
How could I walk alone again?

Awake at night
Pining for my knight
He would want me to live again.

Couples stroll by
I try not to cry
Or wish for things that had not been.

Finding new work
Dreams from the past lurk
It hurts, learning to walk again!

Crutches removed
His provision proved
Slowly I'll learn to walk again.

My heart so raw
Grief a steady gnaw
Lord, show me how to live again.

Whole is my goal
Mind, body and soul
Drawing near to the Lord again.

We may not ride
Again on this side
I'll keep walking, 'til we meet again.

Lola Chiantaretto

Sweet talk

Words so soft and tender,
Spoken with tone, gentle, and kind.
Words not said to his sweetheart,
But, rather shared with his bovine.

Feeding cattle together isn't easy,
I drive the truck and he's behind,
Tossing hay and giving directions-
I believe he thinks I'm blind!

He shouts at me and coos to them,
"TURN HERE!" "Come, Boss,"
As to whom he is addressing,
I am never at a loss.

Now please don't judge my husband,
Or tell me that's just not right
Because when this day is over,
I'm the one he'll kiss goodnight!

Andrea Waitley

GOD'S BOUQUETS

He had to ride cattle,
So he asked me to go.
I had no idea
He was planning a show.

He saddled up Chip,
And I rode my mare
My eyes were amazed
At what awaited me there.

Yellow daisies, purple thistle,
And red mallow grew free,
A display of God's glory
And splendor to me.

Now some buy their sweethearts
Flowers from town,
And that is a gesture I'd never put down.
But nothing compares to a late summer day,
When my husband thrills me
With God's lovely bouquets!

Andrea Waitley

65

WHAT COWBOY MEANS

Men have tried to redefine the cowboy
But there are things that can't be changed
You can't change the Chiricahua Mountains
Or the way dirt smells when it rains
And you can't stop the wind from blowin'
And progress from ruinin' what was fine
And you can't make someone a cowboy
And you can't stop the passing of time
He must have a heart the size of the West
And eyes to see past the show
He must have knowledge you can't learn from a book
And sense which way the cattle will go
He must have faith that it will rain
When the long drought threatens his hope
Have a feel for the things of nature
And be a good hand with a rope
He knows how long the grass will last
And if there's water over the next rise
He must know the bawling of the cattle
And all of the reasons why
If you ask him the time of day
He'll tell you by how the shadows look
He must know that time is only borrowed
And read the clouds like a book
And you can't make someone a cowboy
With a Stetson hat, boots, and Levi jeans
You can't make someone a cowboy
Until they understand what cowboy means
Silently you watch him and wonder why he keeps going
On land that he doesn't own, but he keeps on knowing
What belongs to God is only on precious loan.

Kip Calahan Young & Susan Young Warner

Today

The day dawned beautiful and bright
Everything seemed to be so right
Birds were chirping, some were singing
Some were sitting on branches and preening
The trees were all in dressed in rose and white blossom
The world was so breathtakingly awesome!
Deer were bounding in the brook
From the cool clear water a drink they took
Elk stood tall on the mountain top
While the large white tail of a rabbit a'hop
Looked just like a bouncing mop
Antelope watched and gazed at us
Even though we were quiet and made no fuss.
It makes me glad to be alive,
With energy and hope to survive.

Shirley Tecklenburg

Not a suburban housewife

Sometimes, I think I missed my true calling as a suburban housewife. I could totally see myself signing for UPS packages while my husband was at work and Disney Junior blared in the background.

Instead, I live on a remote cattle ranch two and a half hours from town and one hour past mail delivery. Even though I grew up in the country, sometimes I think I'm not cut out for life as a cowboy's wife. I want my children to be clean for longer than a bath. I want to see a tarantula never, instead of on my bathroom floor.

I dream of having real electricity. We live off the grid, so when the power goes out, I must get out of my warm bed—sometimes during a freezing rainstorm—and locate a flashlight, find my husband's boots, then brace myself for the final step.

"Here, take these and go start the generator," I whisper as I shake Jim's shoulder.

"Why? It's the middle of the night."

"I might want to make some microwave popcorn."

"We don't have a microwave."

"I might want to watch TV."

"We don't have cable."

"I might want to read a book."

"Use your flashlight."

I want to know what it's like to buy bananas and have them arrive at my home bright yellow and unbruised. I wonder what it's like to brake smoothly at the stop sign on the corner rather than shift into four-wheel drive in order to make it through the cow pasture on my way to town. I want to walk outside my house in my nightgown to wave at the garbage man and embarrass my kids, not chase the bulls out of the front yard.

I could definitely envision myself driving a shiny SUV that

has never seen a speck of dirt. Maybe a newer model in cobalt blue. In actuality, I do drive an SUV, but it's a '95 Jeep Cherokee. It has a CD player and power nothing, but driving it makes me feel like Indiana Jones.

Plus, out here I have plenty of room to practice my off-road driving skills. Once I got the feel for four-low and made it through a few monster mud puddles, I realized that I could never hack it as a suburban housewife. Next time I see a giant arachnid in my house, I'll just channel my inner Indy and crack a bullwhip at it . . . while screaming for my husband to come kill it, of course.

Jolyn Young

Not a Man's Problem

When I was younger, and a lot more agile,
And lived where the winters were mild,
I never minded a big tall horse,
Or one that got easily riled.

But up north, where the winters are cold,
Where it snows, and it blows and you freeze,
I've got me a gentle, fourteen-two horse,
And my stirrups let out to his knees!

'Cause, up in that far North Country,
Before venturing out in the cold,
I've put on so many layers of clothes,
My body will hardly unfold.

First comes my long-johns and wool socks,
Then a quilted shirt and blue jeans,
A sweater and coat, on top of all this,
And a slicker, of course, is routine.

Chaps or chinks are a must,
Leather gloves all lined inside,
Cowboy boots and overshoes,
My head covered; then I can ride.

When the temperature hovers at thirty,
And the wind is whippin' the snow,
The house feels so warm and cozy inside,
Lord knows I'm not wantin' to go.

But when that cowboy heads for the door,
The horses are ready to haul,
Draggin' my boots won't do any good,
It's no use tryin' to stall.

There's one last bunch of cows to move,
And a storm came in overnight
Yesterday, not one little cloud,
The skies were sunny and bright.

So this change in the weather demands
That my morning be totally free
Of any kind of liquids,
No breakfast coffee for me!

'Cause the last thing in the world I need,
And the thing I dread most of all,
Is gettin' dressed up in all of these clothes,
Then havin' to heed nature's call.

I try movin' out of the wind,
But it follows wherever I go.
And when I'm finally down to bare skin,
It's feelin' like twenty below!

My chaps are now 'round my ankles,
My jeans somewhere 'neath my knees
My long-johns won't go any lower,
As I squat in the lee of some trees.

The wind blows the snow, and everything else,
But you can't move hobbled like that
To even get up, you're so stiff from the cold,
You need to be half acrobat.

I had to take off my gloves
To get undone for this feat
And by now my fingers are so darn numb
The buckles and buttons won't meet.

By the time I get put back together,
And make my way up on my horse,
The cowboy is bringin' the last of the cows
Lookin' plumb disgusted, of course!

Bein' a man, he can't figure,
What would cause this long a delay
In the meantime, I'll just keep working
On learning to "hold it" all day.

Carole Jarvis

It's my life

I've been a ranch wife for many, many years
And I was country born and raised
I feel so blessed that it's been that way
And not city livin' instead.

Did you ever ride a bus many miles home from school
And walk into a house filled with the smell
Of light bread bakin' in an old wood stove
And quench your thirst with water drawn from a well?

Wake up to the sound of the rain comin' down
On a tin roof while you lay there in your bed
And the freshness that comes with the mornin' sun
Bringin' thoughts of peace and tranquility to your head?

Have you ever rode horseback to the top of a mountain
Where you could see the beauty for miles below?
Or got up early some mornin' before a track was made
On a pure white blanket of snow.

Have you ever seen a red tail hawk
As he searches out his prey
While you watch the sun come up over the mountain
Sendin' sunbeams out across the way.

Did you ever sit and watch the moon rise
In peaceful solitude miles from town?
Or watched a beautiful sunset in the evenin'
With nothin' but nature's peaceful sound?

Seen the cattle out there grazin'
Watched their calves as they run and play
Heard the sound of the coyotes howlin'
As it just begins to break day.

I feel so blessed to have experienced all of these things,
Yes, this and much, much more.
And I feel thankful for havin' been privileged to live
Where many of God's beautiful creations were
        right there in my back door.

It's true ranch life is hard and the hours are long
Many sacrifices have to be made most every day
But this is my life, the life that I love
And I can't imagine wantin' it any other way.

Daisy Dillard

Pass to hell

Never underestimate the strength of a ranch wife
She is close friends with fear, loneliness, and well hid pain
She commits to a "jack of all trades" title in this life
Leaving little time for her heart's desires to reign

She will doctor his best horse or calve out the heifer
Stay nights alone with the kids for weeks and weeks on end
She troubleshoots the pivot while battling Zephyr
And still picks up the phone when needed by her best friend

Somedays it's a Bible verse, others a harsh curse word
An Ian Tyson classic or a Nickelback tune
She responds without emotion or with her heart stirred
She'll party or nap, high noon or under the full moon

She's the wild fire with the ever-changing wind
Do not back burn her and expect it to turn out well
Her strength makes her resilient against those who pretend
Fear her who's survived it yet still buys a pass to hell

Jessica Hedges

ICE FLOWERS

With ragged fingernail I scrape
lacy swirls of ice from window
see cows in winter's landscape
backs hunched, frosted white with snow
waiting for me to feed them, I know.

Splash diesel on kindling splinters
wait, impatient for red glow
curse the cold and pain of winters'
memories recalled from long ago
wakened by this new fallen snow.

Freezing winds twist and whittle
any warmth the sun can bequeath
leaving my bones bound and brittle
like frozen grass buried beneath
cured and preserved in its own sheath.

Slowly melting like daydreams
ice flowers slide down the window
The years do not change it seems
hungry cattle still wait in snow
waiting for me to feed them, I know.

Deanna Dickinson McCall

My soul is there, outside

The sun came up over my kitchen sink
The quiet house started to stir
The coffee was perkin' and biscuits brown
And I can hear the house cat purr.

As I open the door to the chicken coop
The hens file out one by one
Cluckin' softly as they scratch for bugs
Under the new mornin' sun.

The horses nicker for morning hay
And the milk cow moos for relief
The cowboys stir for that first mornin' cup
With a chaser of bacon, biscuits and eggs.

After breakfast is over
The men all head outside
Each one catches his mount for the day
Pickin' the horses they'll ride.

I watch as I clean up the kitchen
Wash the dishes and put them away
My heart is rememberin' another time
Back in my younger days.

A time when I caught my horses
And saddled up for the ride
And though my body's in the kitchen
My soul is there outside.

Janet Moore

Hollyhocks

Hollyhocks and old ranch wives both thrive on so little care
Bringing beauty to barren places,
Enduring year after year.
They're at it again, the old men, reliving their glory days
Cattle they caught, horses they made,
Cowboy pride, cowboy ways.
An old wife moves among them, invisible but for coffee pot
They don't see her leave, or care that she goes
To smile and tend her hollyhocks.
She shares no glory stories, her choice was supporting role
Freeing her man to follow his call,
She felt privileged just to fill a hole.
She was the one left to hold the gather;
For hours she'd highpoint alone
Till she often wondered if they'd changed the plan,
Forgot her and gone on home.
Relegated to ride drag with the little kids,
She ate dust while planning meals
No good hand could be spared for that,
He wouldn't even remember how it feels.
She did up the jobs left undone by men
With better things to do,
Doctored horses, milked the cow, ran the kids to school.
She brushed the bucket babies
The way mother cows lick their calves
Till they glowed and gained on her tender care
She never nurtured by halves.
Now her waist is thick, her hair is thin,
And her knees are stiff when she walks.
A solitary figure out in the yard,
Humming and tending her hollyhocks.
Hollyhocks and old ranch wives, both thrive on so little care
Bringing beauty to barren places,
Enduring, year after year.

Audrey Hankins

Chicken for Dinner

Dogs on an outfit can be a big help, or big trouble! Most big outfits won't let you have your own dogs. Or your own horses for that matter. However, one particular place we worked we were living in a trailer between headquarters and another small house where a Mexican family lived. They had a little flock of chickens that provided eggs and meat for them on a consistent basis.

Somewhere in the mix of things, my husband came home with a Catahoula pup that he was overly proud of . . . but surely you can imagine where this story is headed. That pup was fond of chicken for dinner.

I tried everything I ever heard of to break that dog from killing their chickens. Finally they built a better fence around the coop, and we all made a diligent effort to keep the dog at a safe distance from their place.

However, one morning I heard my son screaming at the pup in a high pitched voice, and then he burst into the room with eyes wide and yelled, *"That dam' dog's got a chicken in his mouth and won't let 'im go!"*

"You hush that kind of talk right now."

"Well, he does!" was the crisp retort.

Completely at my wits end as to what to do about the problem, in complete exasperation I stepped to the closet. Reaching in, I took out a .22 rifle, stepped to the porch, took a deep breath, and aimed at all I could see of a runaway dog with a chicken flapping and squawking in its mouth. I shot the dog right through the heart. He went down, the chicken flapped its way back to the coop expressing her indignation, and I went to find the Mexican to enlist his help dealing with the dog.

Personally, I had all I could do dealing with telling my husband about the ordeal when he came home looking for his dog.

As months went by, the family living at headquarters found us another Catahoula pup, which they brought over, ironically, the same evening the Mexican family brought us a stewed chicken for dinner! My husband smiled, thanked the family for dinner, and winked at the man with the pup in his arms, saying, "Sorry, I can't take that pup. My wife kills dogs."

We kept the dog; he lived to be fourteen.

Sequent Bodine

THIS TOWN

I love this town.
Not the asphalt streets or three story buildings.
       But the sweet old folks with grit and guts
       Who drove these streets with muddy ruts
       When they were dirt and the town was young.
       Ah, yes . . . I love that town.
I love this town.
Not the grind and grit of downtown noise.
       But the birds that sing in early spring
       And build their nests in pine bough swings
       Until their babies call and sing.
       Mmmmm . . . I love that town.
I love this town.
Not the politicians who rake and take.
       But when the rain falls sweet and slow
       And the fragrance fills my heart and soul
       With a peace and calm I rarely know.
       I love that town.
I love this town.
Not traffic that jams and grinds to a halt.
       But in garden's early evening glow
       When folks are home and it's easy go
       Where old men sit to laugh and crow.
       Oh, how I love that town.
I love this town.
Not where the hills hold glass and gloss.
       But the flags that wave over veterans brave
       And the hills that are filled with Indian graves
       Where cattle and horses and horseback men
       Left tracks that are blown away again.
       Oh, yes . . . I love that town.

Sally Harper Bates

THE ROMANTIC LIFE OF A COWBOY'S WIFE

Ah! The glamour and romantic life of a cowboy's wife,
At least the movies portray it so.
But I thought I should tell you just a few of the things
That those movie folks don't show.

Maybe milkin' a cow's romantic and glamorous
When he says he has other things he has to do
And he's sure you won't mind
If he leaves the milkin' to you.

Never mind she ain't the gentlest of cows
One that's just slightly hard to milk
And when you least expect it, she kicks the bucket
And you wind up wearin' most of the milk.

Then sometimes you get to hold the twitch
On some fight'n horse he's tryin' to shoe
Well, you're the only one around
So what else is he supposed to do.

And there's the time you just finished moppin'
    the kitchen and bathroom floors
And it makes you feel so good
To see them so shiny and clean
Lookin' the way that they should.

But about the time you're finished
And you're thinkin' they look so neat
In comes your cowboy
With manure all over his feet.

Oh, this is just too much
"Why didn't you pull your boots off?" you yell
But by now he's gone through the livin' room
And the carpet'll have signs to tell.

"Where's all those papers that were in here?
I need the papers on the horse I sold that guy last week."

He hollers as he goes through the livin' room
And you're standin' there grittin' your teeth.

"Oh, you mean the ones scattered and piled all over in there?
I threw 'em in the trash, I guess.
I tried to get you to sort through 'em and put 'em away.
And I got tired of lookin' at the mess."

He started lookin' through the trash,
Mumblin' and gruntin', and I thought I heard him swear.
Then after a few minutes his grumblin' stops
So I supposed he found 'em in there.

After he finds the papers and leaves
The cleanin' process starts again
But this time you're gonna' lock the door
So he can't just come traipsin' in.

It does have its romantic side though
Somewhat like the movies show
But there's two sides to every story
And I just thought you ought to know.

You're still fumin' when you hear him holler,
"I'm gonna' take a drive, 'ya wanna go?"
You're thinkin' "I should stay home and show him."
But in about 5 seconds you're out the door.

Then on the way back there's a beautiful sunset
And it's been a wonderful afternoon
You take a deep breath and think to yourself
That this day has ended too soon.

When each day's hard work is over and he kisses you goodnight
You know there's really never a moment of doubt
That you bein' this cowboy's wife
Is what happiness is all about.

Daisy Dillard

Chosen

There will always be horses and cattle
As long as this old earth stands
And the men and women of integrity
Still abide where a man's a man.

Cowhands, and that's women too, sir,
Breathe free in God's great outdoors
Seeing His glory in sunrise and sunset
Riding land where the eagle soars.

Hard work it is, but blessed indeed,
A cowhand rides there with pride
For God honors those who steward His land,
Leads them over the Great Divide.

Bertha Monroe

Music Mountain Cowgirl

"Roll out of bed, Sis, time to feed!"

Roll out? These Navajo blankets are weighing me down till I can't even roll over, how does Dad think I can roll out? I slowly open my eyes and try to sit up.

I can't believe it! Little lines of snow stretch across the red wool blanket. I remember the wind pushing stronger last night, and I guess it blew the snow through the cracks in the wall of my little lean-to bedroom. I shiver, breathe deep; my breath freezes.

That was the start of my day on the Music Mountain Ranch one winter. Some days were hot and dry, some were windy, sometimes it would rain, and there were some winters we were snowed in and the helicopters dropped hay for the cattle.

No electricity or running water. Our house was really an old line camp. A kitchen, living room with fireplace, and one bedroom. A lean-to for my bedroom. My brothers had bunkbeds in the porch that Dad enclosed.

We were all the help Mom and Dad had to run this outfit. When we first bought it, it was full of wild cattle.

The days were long, and we rode hard every day. Sometimes we camped out; some nights the boys and I rode home in the dark while Mom and Dad hauled a load of cattle to the sale.

That's how I grew up. That's how I learned to love the Music Mountains near Kingman, Arizona. It was a hard life, but when you love something the way we did, the hard fades and the easy kicks in.

Then I fell in love with a Texas/New Mexico cowboy, got married, and went from the wild ride on the Musics to a wild ride from Arizona to Hawaii and Canada and a few stops in between before landing back in Arizona.

We saw a lot of neat country, and he worked on some great ranches while I raised five children. I was raised horseback; I wanted to raise my kids horseback. But most of the outfits didn't want wives or kids helping out except maybe in the branding corral. So I took up photographing everything I could.

At some point, we knew we wanted to have our own outfit instead of working for someone else for cowboy wages. We prayed about it and headed back to the Music Mountains and leased the old ranch from the Hualapai Tribe, who now owned it. We had no retirement account and never could keep savings past the point of new truck tires, so we had to borrow everything we needed. Including horses. Most big outfits didn't want you to own or bring personal horses with you, so we didn't own a one.

We were told more than once that we'd never make it.

We moved onto the place in January. The buildings had all fallen down, so we set up our tepee and made camp. A half barrel became our heat and cook-stove; what we needed was kept in the horse trailer. Most of our belongings we left in storage.

We borrowed money and bought some heifers from Mark Goswick. Shipped them to one of our water lots, and turned them out. Added some black bulls, and there we had the beginning of our own herd.

Of course, the horses you borrow are usually not the ones that are keepers, or no one would loan them to two people on a rough old ranch! Without further comment, you can imagine the kind of rides we put in, keeping care of that little bunch of cattle.

The corrals were in as bad a shape as the headquarter buildings, so we had a lot of work to get accomplished. Nothing was up to being able to work cattle in. Some cattle from the tribe had crawled through the boundry fence, and I prayed for God to send angels to help us get them into our barely standing water lot, through a very sketchy crowding pen, and into the trailer.

One morning shortly after we moved onto the place, not into any kind of home, we woke up to a foot of snow. It was well below zero several mornings, and the tepee we were living in was as cold inside as it was outside. I nailed old tin to some posts alongside an old shed for a wind break, moved the barrel and a rickety wooden table inside with us. At least it was out of the wind. But, it could get smoky, and with no roof, quite often we had snow in our makeshift kitchen.

We camped out like that for a couple of years, and many times I wondered if we'd lost our minds. But the love for what we were doing kept us hooked in.

After those two tough years, a friend brought lumber from a mill he owned and helped us build a one-room house. We built it around the old fireplace which was all that was still standing of the house I grew up in. Dan was day working, and winter was moving in, so I found a roll of heavy plastic and covered the windows. I hung a big blanket on the door and moved in. Never was that old fireplace so appreciated. I will probably never live that down.

We finally got the cattle all paid for, the cabin actually is a bit like a house, though has not one bit of insulation, so winter is winter and summer is hot. We still pack our water in and still have an outhouse. My cook-stove is a camp stove.

We still have the dream of owning our own outfit. But that is in God's good timing. For now, I'm living the life that started out here many years ago, and it is a blessing! Horseback on the mountains, riding the malapai rock piles, the steep canyons, and seeing cattle here again. That's always a good day.

Dry years, snowed in, rain in dirt tanks and hot days, just like before.

Terry Crowley

* Editors note: Just to clarify, this isn't from the early 1900'. It's 2018 and Terry is still living in her Music Mountain home! She works in Kingman and Dan does day-work as they continue working together to accomplish their dream. I have always admired her tenacity and guts! She is truly a woman of the West, and her life stands as a beacon to those who have toughed it out and been proud to live life Facing West.

Sandstone ... O RO

In the rugged mountains of Yavapai County in Arizona, nestled around Mount Hope lies an old Spanish land grant. The brand they run is close to a hundred years old, the O RO. Better known as the RO's. This historic ranch still runs a wagon fall and spring, with five camps scattered to the far reaches of this vast piece of country. There in these humble abodes reside the care takers of bovine prodigy. These elusive "bovine technicians" roam the country side providing care for the bovine species that provide numerous products for public consumption.

The women who reside with these "technicians" have tenacity running through their veins thicker than blood. These vast regions are testing grounds of an age old tradition ... the glue that holds these females in place despite the hardships that come their way.

Sandstone is the closest camp to headquarters tucked up under the east side of Mount Hope. A Windmill provided water for the house and livestock. This was a rare camp that boasted a fenced in yard with lush vines, a smattering of fruit trees, small garden area to provide fresh food for family, and even a small patch of grass that provided cool comfort under the shade of an ancient cedar tree.

Even though it was not on the "grid" it was a very pleasant place to reside as it wasn't too far from headquarters and only a couple of hours from town during good weather. Thus, providing a fairly comfortable abode for this small family.

Sometime during April of 1982, the bovine technician assigned to this camp had decided to depart the ranch and told me that he was going to visit his brother and would be back in a couple of days. He took the only vehicle to be had, but that was not considered too much of a problem as it was a customary practice. Waving him off in a cloud of dust, I turned back to the house with thoughts of daily chores, horses to feed two small children to care for, and a generator that would have to be started if it was to be used.

I was most grateful for an old wringer washer with a gas motor that provided something more than a rub-board and a lot of elbow grease for laundry. It had been loaned to me by an older couple who had been good friends with my parents and who lived at the RO headquarters.

The days went by, and the routine of chasing kids, sewing and doing chores left little time for concern at the absence of a vehicle until, two weeks came and went, and the groceries started getting low. Getting rather anxious, I used the radio supplied by the ranch to contact Headquarters and ask them to call the absentee bovine technician's brother and make sure he was on his way home. The manager came back with a message that he had been sick but would be home in a few days.

Pushing hard into week three, this woman was starting to get a burr under her hide. So when the horses came in, they were fed and the gate closed behind them. Amongst the small band of horses was a streak-faced sorrel called "Streaker". He was quiet, easy going, and smooth riding. Having ridden him before, I figured he was a good prospect to help me with my mission.

Our oldest child would turn three in July; her brother was a few months past one. How to transport these youngsters horseback through several wire gates, did not seem to present a problem at the moment, nor was being seven months pregnant an issue in my mind either. Plus, I needed some groceries. They'd have to be packed in flour sacks and tied to the saddle, hopefully without causing too many problems.

I saddled Streaker with an old Porter saddle giving to me by my Dad. It had a low cantle and a large flat saddle horn that made a perfect seat for a small wee son. The low cantle making it easier to swing a leg over for a pregnant woman. The flour sacks were perfect for tucking in a couple of cloth diapers, wet washrag, and a change of clothes for small people. Thus, I felt we were well-prepared for our jaunt.

Leading Streaker up to a stump tall enough to place the stirrup within reach, I clambered aboard with very little grace and rode him around in a few circles to make sure he was in good humor. That being accomplished with little discomfort it was on to step two.

My daughter was a green eyed little pixie with thick brown hair, a willing heart and a mother hen attitude toward her younger brother. She always had a smile and a twinkle in her eye. My dark-haired little boy had shinning eyes, an easy laugh and was his sister's constant companion, following her everywhere, doing all she asked.

Carefully instructing the tiny two year old to lift the one-year old up as high as she could was an easy job to ask of her as she was always happy to be of help. She was just high enough to lift him within reach so that I could pull him up and perch him on the saddle horn. She hopped up on the stump making it an easy swing to settle her behind me, telling her to hold on to the cantle we were off. The pony seemed to understand his job and was taking very good care not to jostle his burden, and that said a lot about this "wagon". It was six and a half miles to Headquarters, not too far a jaunt in this female's mind.

What a beautiful day; the sun was warm, and the days had lengthened enough that we should be able to make it there and back before dark. Our adventure began, and fun was to be had! It had been a long time since I'd enjoyed the sway of a horse's gait, warm sun, and the pleasure of several hours being in the outdoors.

At the top of a long hill, we came to the first of several gates. Feeling confident, I was certain that if we could make it through the first wire gate with no mishaps, the journey was going to go smoothly.

The challenge had arrived; how to get through the wire gate with all of us intact. The task began with shuffling passengers. Swinging the two-year-old down, I handed the boy safely down into her small reaching hands to hold. I gingerly stepped off, noting our transporter was behaving splendidly with his new job. Opening the wire gate, I led the horse through, taking care to keep the little ones from being stepped on. Once through the gate, we found a rock to make our re-mount easier, which was not too difficult as the ground was covered in all sizes of boulders. This little cowpony sidestepped closer to the children and with the help of the two-year-old again, I swung the baby up and then the oldest up behind, establishing a good safe routine.

At the second gate, the baby needed a diaper change. Sweeping off a spot on the ground, to minimize his discomfort, he was laid down and changed into a dry cloth diaper. What to do with the slightly smelly one? Well, no worries, it just got hung on the barbed wire next to the gate to dry and be picked up on the way home, no one the wiser!

The day was getting warmer, and with an easy gait, the pony

rocked the littlest child fast asleep. Keeping up a dialog with the oldest girl was easy, pointing out the quail and rabbits we spotted along the way kept her entertained and awake. My arms being full of the baby and bridle reins, it would have been a task to keep her balanced behind me if she fell asleep.

Two more gates were conquered in the same manner as the first. Headquarters was a welcomed sight. John and Vi Sanders' house was our first stop. Lifting the children down, followed by an awkward dismount, I had to stand still and stretch for a few moments. This small adventure had made the new baby I was carrying rather cranky, and she was letting me know about it.

Tying the faithful, patient, now sincerely appreciated pony up to the yard fence, I gathered the kids, and knocked on the kitchen door. Vi opened the door took one look at me another look at the horse and said, "What the hell are you doing?"

With a sheepish look, I told her that I needed to make a phone call and gather up a few groceries. I am here to tell you Mrs. Vi had some choice words to say to this female. She gathered all of us up and settled us at her kitchen table. Drinks and cookies were set out for all of us.

This precious couple helped me through many adventures and they always opened their home when I came up to headquarters. Potty-breaks, diaper changes and meals were often served in her haven of rest. We always had time to visit, laugh and share stories.

Vi was a short, stocky woman, who could make cowboys shake in their boots. At only five feet tall on her tippy toes, she had jet black hair, and was one of the best cooks that Northern Arizona had ever grown. Her husband Johnny was a tall man with a quick wit and gruff voice, who never failed to pull out the Oreos every time I showed up with the kids, all cleaned up and headed to town. He would chuckle as I had to re-clean them before we were able to settle back into the vehicle. He was well known for being cantankerous and hard to get along with, but nevertheless a good all around hand.

He soon wandered in from the shop with a crooked grin on his face, and said, "So I guess you need to go use the phone."

At my response, he drove me up to the main house so I could make my phone call. Having made my call, and still "hot" under the collar, I had Johnny made a stop by the commissary. We gathered up a few groceries, and then headed back to see how Mrs. Vi was getting along with the two wee ones.

She quite vehemently informed me that under NO circumstances was I going to ride back to Sandstone. She told Johnny to gather up my horse and ride him back for me. He shook his head, muttering under his breath, "Dang wagon widows". But he giggled a bit, gathered up Streaker, and headed south.

Mrs. Vi piled all of us in their single cab truck and home we headed. We got there before Johnny, so we had some more chat-time while I did chores ,fed the kids, and made iced tea for all of us. The babies were tired so it wasn't long before they were laid down for the night and were soon asleep.

Johnny rode off the hill, unsaddled the faithful pony, and came up to the house. We sat down, drank our tea, and had a good visit and a lot of laughs.

As they readied to leave, Johnny turned to me and said, "I have done a lot of things in my day, and seen even more, but by jiminy if you want that diaper back your gonna have to get it your own self."

Jiminell Cook

*Wagon widow is the term used for women who stay home in camp while the cowboys are "out with the wagon." Very few ranches still use an actual cook wagon when they do spring and fall works, but a few do.

Again

At first it was fun, gettin' to ride with you guys.
Then I had to "cowboy up," ignore my screaming thighs.

We rode dark to dark, doctored sick steers with a cold
Mended fence in the hot sun, endured your "helpful scold."

I survived stampedes, rattlesnakes, steep dusty trails,
Camped in our old canvas tepee that billowed like sails.

Learned to rope and spook, to help you get cattle in,
I climbed that darn ol' windmill, got it runnin' again.

I lost my tally, while tryin' to slow the herd
Outran that horned maverick bull,
    Man, how I whipped and spurred!

I fed all your cows, gathered cattle in the snow
I've been jumped by a mad cow, near knocked down by a doe!

Got sun and wind burns, algarita in my chaps
Had coils come tight on my arm, helped you sew a prolapse.

Bucked off more than once, been to the ER twice now,
My oil paints have plumb dried up, but I can turn a cow!

It may sound crazy, but desire still burns within,
If we got a chance, my love, I'd do it all again!

Lola Chiantaretto

COBBLED~UP PEACH COBBLER

A few years back a friend of ours broke his arm just as they were getting ready to start the fall works, and he had a crew coming out to help for a week. He stopped by the house on his way back from town after getting his arm cast, and I could see he was needing help but wasn't wanting to come right out and ask. So I offered to come out three days that week and cook; then I'd leave stuff for them to heat up the other days of the week. He seemed glad to have the help, so I went to the grocery store and did a week's worth of shopping and set to making up dishes that I could deliver and they could heat up.

The first day I really wanted to do up a peach cobbler as I knew it would work for dessert at least two meals. I knew the crust was going to present a problem for me. That was something I had never conquered. But, I found a box of Bisquick, doctored it up with brown sugar and vanilla extract, made it the consistency of a cake batter and poured-er-on.

I finished up the rest of the roast-and-a-pot-of-beans meal with fried taters and green bean cowboy salad. I popped open the oven to see a glob of uncooked batter melted over the top of what was supposed to be peach cobbler. Upping the temp, I cooked it until the boys finished eating. Again, opened the oven door and to my dismay it wasn't looking any better than the time before.

I cranked the heat up to 400 and prayed, told the boys have another cup of coffee and hopefully they'd have dessert in a few minutes. No dice. I finally took it out, spooned their dishes full from the outside edges of the pan where at least the batter was beginning to firm up.

True to form, not one of those cowboys complained a whit, just gobbled up the cobbled up peach cobbler and went on back to work.

About a year later, I had several people over for dinner, and two of the men on the crew brought their families over. I made up my mind I was going to build a peach cobbler to die for! All I can say is, "Pride really does go before a fall." All the excuses in the world don't change the facts. They left knowing full well not to ever expect a decent peach cobbler if they're eating where I'm cooking.

Sally Harper Bates

A FINE OLD TREE

Winter of 1977, my husband was running the O RO Ranch, and we were living in a big house that had tall ceilings. Which was a treat because most cow-camps are small, older houses, with very small rooms.

For months, Mike had been telling our seven and five year olds about a Christmas tree he had spotted when checking cattle and country. He'd say, "Well, gang, I've seen the world's best Christmas tree. It's perfect for a big house with high ceilings."

At last it was time for the tree to come live at our house for a season. He took the kids and made the long trek. It seemed they were gone forever, but finally, nearing dusk, up drives my crew. I waited expectantly with hot chocolate ready, anticipating a fun party at our house that night. They came trudging in with the happy faces I expected.

"Well, Momma," he smiled rather sheepishly. "My perfect tree kind'a fell apart. The more I tried the worse it got. We could only use the top part, and after climbing to cut the top out, I realized it's still too tall."

So, he and his saw went to work. He measured the height, the tall ceilings, stepped back, sized up the trunk several times, and realized he still had a too tall tree. Another sawing episode. Pretty soon the sad little faces of the kids showed clearly their disappointment in what was turning into a "Charlie Brown" Christmas tree.

So as to salvage what was left, he gathered up a lot of the branches, assuring the kids when he got through it would be a marvelous tree. Hammer, nails, a little string here and there. When he finally stood it up in the corner, BAM, down it fell. So, as any good cowboy would do in the old days, off he went to the barn for baling wire. Only you older readers will remember the value of baling wire. Much more useable than the twine they use today.

He literally tied the tree to our walls, wiring it to nails run through cracking plaster, making holes everywhere. But our tree was going up one way or another! It was pitifully ashamed of its bare nakedness, with its glorious branches hacked and stacked. But stand it did!

93

With hearts aflame, our crew pulled out the decorations. Here was an apparent second flaw in the making. We had very few ornaments, and this tree would have required the amount it took to decorate the County Courthouse in Prescott!

Never faltering, we made the best of a bad situation. We popped corn and strung it on long pieces of thread, and made some homemade decorations out of what ever we could gather up. After all, it's not like we could run to town and get "stuff". It was a two hour drive over muddy roads this time of year. And money wasn't exactly pouring out of our pockets. Even foreman wages were sparse in the ranching industry.

I have many memories through the years, of lots and lots of different trees that graced our homes. There have been some super ones . . . but this is the one I remember most. It held my first realization of the determination of my cowboy husband, and the ingenuity that my children produced creating their own celebration.

I wouldn't trade that memory for the finest tree in all the world.

Billie Jo McFarland

Notes from my journal

November 22, 2015

Moon and stars over high
Light brightens the red canyon walls
Evening quickly turning cold.
So quiet now, only the sound of the river
Slowly wandering down stream.
With cottonwoods now in their winter attire.

July 23, 2015

Like a spotlight on a star actor in the last act of a play,
Light from the setting sun,
    shines through the dark clouds to the east
        onto the red rock cliffs.
Reflection of sienna and yellow ochre sparkle in the river below.
A cool breeze rustles through cottonwoods and desert willows.
Bats and swallows fill the sky in search of their desert meal.
Then, too soon, the light and color are gone,
    like the final curtain coming down on stage.

Fall of 2015

Cottonwood leaves flutter
Down in the fall breeze
Like wistful yellow butterflies.

November 2, 2015

Evening walk, dogs running and playing,
A chill in the air
Crickets play their music as birds say goodnight
Horses grazing
The sound of the river flowing by cottonwoods
Not quite gold.
Getting dark, turning back, the end of day.
Tomorrow leaves will be gone.

December 10, 2017

Mourning doves, blush gray,
Fill a dark winter mesquite tree.
Look like ornaments on Christmas Day.

December 28, 2017

She looks, and sniffs my pockets
Her eyes light up when I pull out carrots
Cut up into bite-size pieces.
I hold them out to her, one by one.
From my palm she reaches,
Her soft lips carefully picking them up.
She searches for the next piece.
With a disappointed look
When she realizes,
There are no more.
    (For Savannah July 3, 1992—March 15, 2018)

Karen Perkins

Anorexic Christmas Tree

"You've got to be kidding me! That's the most anorexic Christmas tree I've ever seen!" Then he laughed that hearty burst that expresses true, deep amusement. A "neighbor" had stopped by on his way home, a ranch sixty miles up the road.

I bristled, "Listen, don't you be laughin' at my tree! That's a beautiful tree, and one that holds all my ornaments with loving care. Besides, it's the only one I could fit in this little house."

The object of my affection was the top portion of a century plant, better known in my book of southwestern plants as an agave. Its branches were sparse, dried limbs from a native cactus found throughout Arizona in rocky country where barely anything else will survive. Maybe some scraggly cedars and piñon, native grasses, a smattering of prickly pear cactus, and usually lots and lots of malapais boulders.

We'd moved into that tiny little house with intentions of adding on sometime in the future, but what few pieces of furniture were to be had simply filled up the twelve by fourteen area we called the living room. The kitchen was about the same size, but counter tops and refrigerator used up what space was left over after we added a four by four table and two chairs. One room to sleep in and a bathroom with a linen closet were the rest of the home we found resting on four acres at the foot of a giant granite mountain. We killed seven rattle snakes in the yard the first year.

It was four days away from Christmas, the first time in my life there would be no family around a table full of turkey and fixin's. I wasn't interested in decorating or planning for anything special. I was depressed, dreading that day without children around a fragrant piñon tearing away paper and bows. I stood at the sink, washing dishes, feeling quite sorry for myself.

Off in the distance stood that dried up old century plant. I realized it was wide at the bottom, narrow at the top, and was somewhat similar in shape to a Christmas tree. I dried my hands, procured a saw, and walked out in the pasture to gather my tree. It took some doing, but it wasn't long until I had that scrawny example standing in the corner by the window. I trotted out a small box of ornaments and triumphantly displayed my treasure for all to see.

Even those who found my little tree quite amusing.

Sally Harper Bates

DINNER BELL

1985 fall works . . . Mike Landis was boss, Double O Ranch, Seligman, Arizona. The cook got sick, so Mike asked if I'd cook at the wagon. Mike's son-in-law had sent a mule over to Mike so he could get him over some "attitude" and they thought the fall wagon would help him. His name was Ruban.

Every day the crew went to work about daylight, but by late morning, Ruban would start bellowin'. Soon I figured out the crew was heading back into camp. So, I started the coffee every day with Ruban just a singin' in the breeze, and coffee was always good and hot when they arrived.

He was sure a silly lookin' thing all stirred up, big ol' ears straight out, eyes glued to the horizon. I couldn't ever see what he was a pointing to; I just knew they were comin'.

Ol' Ruban sure made me look good! I always had dinner ready when they hit camp! I'd never cooked for a wagon crew before, but the men thought I was doin' real good. They gave me lots of help, choppin' wood, helping with dishes, etc. They were all great gentlemen.

A couple of days into the works, Twister asked me how I knew to start the coffee so it was always hot and fresh when they hit camp.

"Well, it's Ruban," I told him. "He hollers, sings, and carries on every day about 30 minutes before the crew hits camp."

He was my pard that fall, pretty cheap entertainment. That was a great crew to work with, Mike Landis, Chip Dixon was the Jigger, John McGrew, Cecil Bryant, Twister, Peter Davis and Shorty . . . and of course my dinner bell, Ruban.

Sandy Heller

Ranch Kids

Folks seem to think that there's a clear divide
Only two categories the whole nation wide
But I'm here to tell you, there's more than country and city
Fans of folks other than Luke Bryan and P Diddy
There's another group of kids who don't live in town
And if you call them rednecks they might take ya' down.
They are the ranch kids, you know the ones
They've got sweat stains on their hats and drive beater trucks
They hunt and they fish and they'll even wear camo
But they'll bring in 4x4 muleys wearin' plaid flannel
They ride and rope for a living and still think it's fun
And try to avoid mechanic'n till the baler won't run.
They live down wash-board roads and are used to generator power.
Cow-camp, outhouses, and weeks without a real shower
Can work by kerosene light, mend or make their own tack
Cook on cast iron, shovels, sage brush sticks, open fire snacks.
They were horseback before they learned to walk
Were swinging ropes before they could talk
Driving before they could see over the dash
And working long hours before seeing any cash.
When you say 'oysters' they don't think of sea food
And if you call it a 'lasso' they'll call you a dude
They work with their hands, their heads, and their hearts
They milk cows, gather eggs, and get the tractor to start.
They're either taught at home, or with the three neighbor kids
They call cowboy hats "palm leafs," "sky pieces" or "lids,"
They own new boots but still wear the patched pair
And ride their 4-H steers all over the county fair
Cell service is rare and going to town is a big deal
Chicken is a vegetable, rarely an entire meal.
They grew up on sagebrush, grease wood, and juniper trees
They are what happens when Mommas have cowboy babies.

Randi Johnson

MARCH WINDS

There's laundry to do and breakfast to get
These kids have a big appetite
And if the wind don't tear the sheets off the line
We'll sleep in fresh linens tonight

We're calving heifers and workin' all hours
They like the dark of the night
And the wind beats the chill down into my bones
But those babes are a beautiful sight.

The wind caught the screen door and broke it clean off
The shingles blew off of the shed
Sometimes I walk backward to get where I'm going
No wonder I can't get ahead!

I don't even think about wearin' a dress
Except for service on the Lord's day
Then I'm holdin' my skirt down and loading up kids
While my Sunday school notes blow away

Sometimes I think it will blow me away
I wonder just when it will end
The weatherman says it will die down tonight
Then tomorrow will come up again

But, soon will come summer along with the heat
We'll be checking cattle one day
With that windmill not turning, oh I'll be a-yearning
For the wind will come blow me away!

The wind is as wild as a filly in springtime
Blows like a prairie typhoon
The windmill keeps time like a toe tappin' fiddler
And the tumbleweeds dance to her tune

Jean Prescott / Yvonne Hollenbeck

HUGS WELCOME HERE!

It's wondrous what a hug can do!
A hug can cheer you when you're blue
A hug can say, "I love you so."
Or, "Gee, I hate to see you go!"
A hug is "Welcome back again!"
And, "Great to see you!"
Or, "Where've you been?"
A hug delights, and warms, and charms.
A hug can soothe a small child's pain,
And bring a rainbow after rain.
"The Hug" . . . there's just no doubt about it,
We could scarcely survive without it!
It must be why God gave us arms.
Hugs are great for fathers and mothers
Sweet for sisters, swell for brothers.
And chances are some favorite aunts
Love them more than potted plants.
Kittens crave them. Puppies love them.
Heads of state are not above them.
A hug can break the language barrier
And make the dullest day seem merrier!
No need to fret about the store of 'em
The more you give,
The more there are of 'em.
So, stretch those arms without delay,
Give some one a hug today!

*Western women sometimes live fifty or more miles from their
closest neighbor. Hearing a vehicle crossing a nearby cattle guard
signals welcome visitors. Hugs are always profuse when this event
occurs.

Shirley Tecklenburg

My Horse, "Bugs"

In the spring of 1960, I was four years old. My parents took me up to the big corrals by the bridge over the Verde River. They told me to close my eyes, and when I was finally allowed to open them, there stood my present from my great uncle, Ben. An old, but very nice looking bay with white on his forehead. He had been my great uncle's cow-horse, but now he was mine … my very own!

I think he was as happy to get me as I was to get him. He had a big hollow place near his neck and shoulder. When he was younger he scratched himself and got screwworms in the wound. They had eaten out part of his neck. After being doctored, he healed up fine, and the wound never bothered him. Hence, the name, "Bugs."

He was kind and gentle and handled like a champion! After a few months passed, Mama decided that I could ride Bugs off by myself. She saddled him up for me, threw me up on him, and tied my reins in a knot so I wouldn't lose them. She warned me to be sure to stay close to the house where she could watch me. She also said, "Now, don't you go down there by the river where those cows are bedded down in the sand."

My heart did a double jump because she had said the magic word … "Cows!"

"Okay, Mam, I won't." But as soon as she walked inside, Bugs carried me straight to the cattle. I couldn't wait to start working them the way I had watched Daddy, Grandpa, and the cowboys so many times.

When we got near them, I started yelling, "Ho Ho" and slapping my leg with the reins. Some of the cows jumped up and Bugs went to work. Trying to cut them back, he was ducking and diving like a seasoned cutting horse. But too much of that, and PLOP, I was in the sand wondering what had happened, and if Bugs had run away. But when I turned around, there he was right behind me. The minute I fell off; he had stopped!

I dusted myself off and climbed back up into the saddle. After that, I figured they'd had enough workin' for the day, and we headed home. Mama had seen it all.

That summer Bugs and I got to ride with Dad, Mom, Mike McFarland, and Curt Wells in Prescott's Frontier Days Fourth of July Parade. I felt so happy to be in the special parade on my cow-pony. It wasn't often I got to go to town, let alone ride in a parade.

That year it seemed summer went on forever, but finally fall came and school had taken my older cousins away. They were quite a bit older than I, but I didn't understand why I couldn't go to school too. My grandma had been a school teacher, and she and Mother decided that a few times a week I could ride Bugs the mile up to Grandma's house and we would play school.

Mama made me a big canvas bag for all my school supplies. She would hand me my bag, I'd put the handles over the horn, and off we'd go. About a half a mile up the road was a gate, and on those days Daddy would put a loose rope around the gate so I could open and close it.

When I got to Grandma's house, I would tie Bugs loosely to the fence, Grandma would greet me and invite me in. Then I would sit at a little school desk she had kept over the years. After an hour or so, she'd have enough of playing school, and she'd send me on home.

Another year came and went. When Daddy came to me the fall of '62 to tell me that Bugs had died, I was heart broken! Then in November I came home from school to find that my great uncle Ben had passed away.

I cried for them for the longest time. Somehow I decided that perhaps God needed a good cow-man and his horse.

Karen Perkins

**These days who would ever think to put a four-year-old on a horse and turn them loose. Yet most ranch kids are helping gather cattle at the tender ages mentioned above.

PRAIRIE FIRE

Fire thrust intense orange, hungry fingers high against the inky sky and rode the crest of the hill on the other side of the county road. Anna's eyes stung. Her throat ached. Vehicles with their tanks of water in the back sprayed the flames. Another tractor joined Neil, plowing a firebreak. In the distance, men looked like black stick figures silhouetted in the wavering glow that lit the sky like a sunrise. The heat flushed Anna's face.

She grasped several soaked gunnysacks, climbed the ladder, and spread them over the roof. One eye on the fire, Anna climbed up and down the ladder. Then she watched in horror as the wind switched direction. As if sprouting glowing wings, the fire jumped the road. Now it was headed their way.

"No!" Anna slid down the ladder, missing several rungs. She ran inside, scooped up two-year-old Monica, and raced to the Ford. The engine ground but wouldn't start. Anna pumped the gas pedal furiously, praying out loud, "Help me, Lord, help me." She got out and turned the crank. Nothing. Sweat poured down her back.

Then she shifted the car into neutral, and panting like an old dog, ran around to the back of the car. Anna pushed with all her strength. Her feet slid in the dust. She dashed to the driver's side as the car began to roll.

Anna grabbed the door, jumped inside, and shifted the transmission into low gear. She held her breath as the momentum forced the engine to turn over. After a few reluctant coughs and sputters, it caught. She pushed the choke in and pumped the accelerator until the motor began to run smoother.

She floor-boarded the gas pedal until the old car jounced across the prairie. Anna stopped the car on a hill about a mile to the east of the fire, hands nearly paralyzed on the steering wheel. Her whole body shook. She sat, eyes closed, taking deep ragged breaths until she could collect herself. Then she took Monica in her arms and got out of the car, patting her daughter's back and murmuring to her.

They watched the men struggle to turn the fire. Just as they started another fire line, the wind gave a violent push and the fire jumped over. Men beat at the burning brush and grass with wet gunnysacks, trying to contain the spread. The wildfire twisted and turned, a living entity, consuming the dry prairie grasses.

Anna twisted her ruined skirt in one fist. Would they lose their pastureland and their house, too?

She wanted to scream in her helplessness. Those few men couldn't fight this terrible force of nature. Tears cascaded down her cheeks. All the hard work she and Neil had done, the cold winter, the calves they had saved and nurtured, the hay they'd stacked—all could be gone in a matter of minutes. She hugged Monica tighter against her chest.

Neil and the other tractor driver drove around the fire to plow yet another firebreak. The flames seemed to reach out for them. Jack rabbits scurried from under the sagebrush.

Anna could barely breathe.

The flames reached the firebreak and finding no dry fuel to consume, veered to the west, and as suddenly as it had come from the north, it roared up and over the hill—away from the ranch. Anna felt a few raindrops mingle with the tears on her face and ran laughing back to the car.

She watched for another hour, half-afraid the wind would turn again and bring the fire back. The rain pattered on the car roof intermittently at first and then came down in earnest. She breathed deeply.

Their home was safe.

Heidi M. Thomas

*This story is an excerpt from the novel *Seeking the American Dream,* based on the author's mother. The fire scene is a compilation of experiences of ranchers living on the prairies of eastern Montana.

CHEETOS

He's only two years old
but he already knows what a Cheeto is.

Knows what an orange powdered cheese-food corn puff is
but has never pulled a carrot from the dark earth,
washed it off in the garden hose,
crunched into tender sweetness.

The words corporate culture
make a scream in my soul;
I wish for more black dirt,
more rain,
more imperfect carrots,
sun-warmed cherry tomatoes,
more fat cucumbers with prickles on them.

All of the two-year-olds in the world this morning,
tucked away in their square containers,
insulated from weather
and dirt
and cats with stickers in their toes
and earthworms that would squirm in tiny hands
and wind that would bite their cheeks
and overzealous dogs that would knock them down
on their diapered bottoms,
eat sanitary chemicals,
unwrapped from plastic
served by caretakers,

Already bought,
homogenized,
recognizing that cheetah on the package
and the chemical burn on the tongue.

Amy Hale Auker

Bovine-ology

Now cows, they are amazing
Just look at them out there grazing
Their three jobs they do them well
From the day they're born to the day they sell

All their brain cells in one place
Beef to raise that has good taste
Get out and work, find plenty to eat
Procreate; keep 'em safe. See, all nice and neat.

But the male of the species I'd have to say
God put together in a different way
Brain cells? Well, He gave them three
One for each job, you see

There's one in the brainpan called survive
Says do what you must to stay alive
They only work a few months a year
The rest spent shaded up, water near

The other two, that's another story
I'll tell you here without being gory
They're somewhat lower and a bit further back
They're kept together in a handy sack

The one on the left is where decisions are made
It rules common sense throughout the day
When to eat and when to drink
When to fight and when to shrink

The one on the right? It's a seasonal hooker
It says, "Heeeyyyy baby, you're a looker."
This one's the powerhouse; it rules the coop
Throws common sense and survival for a loop

But there's a monkey-wrench in this exchange
A spring time tradition out here on the range
Where you take bull energy and convert it to steak
Yes, that's right, a steer is what you make

It takes away the "Hey baby" and "Oooooo"
But it takes the other one with it too
The most hapless, hopeless, helpless of critters
Are bovines whose brain cells have become fritters

They'll wad up in a corner full of thirst
Stand there for days, too chicken to be first
Not known to be the greatest of thinkers
Hey, turn right, go eighty feet; there's the drinker

They'll walk a fence for days on end
Just to turn around and walk it again
Want them to go south? They'll go north
Or simply run back and forth

They're extremes of frustration and entertainment
We're always working on their containment
It happens in the spring each year
I'll swear there's nothing dumber that a fresh weaned steer

Mary Matli

THE LESSON

Leathered hands, arthritic and broken
Caressed the strings of the worn old saddle
Nails were split and callouses formed
As he pushed and pulled and pressed and reformed.

"This one's for you" was the message he gave
As his great-grandson watched, eyes ablaze
The admiration hung in the air
As I watched and heard what passed twixt the pair.

"Why do you do it like that, Grampa?"
"Just watch, and see, use your eyes and your brain."
Was all the wrinkled old man replied
As he twisted and platted and measured again.

The razor sharp knife split the leather with ease
Then the second string was braided back through
And repeated to form the knot so tight
Then he shifted his weight on the wobbly stool.

The younger grew quiet, his eyes like a hawk
As he worshipped, and watched, and he gleaned
Not a word passed between as the lesson ensued
An old saddle remade, and then cleaned.

"It's yours now, young man. Keep it oiled and clean,
As you gather and ride to the cattle
One thing left to say, one thing I will add,
Whatever may come, whatever may go,
          don't ever . . . sell your saddle."

Sally Harper Bates

I RODE WITH MY COWBOY LOVE TODAY

I rode with my cowboy love today, my heart so full of pride
I never thought I'd experience again
Him riding by my side

How time has been a friend and foe, my truth to be revealed.
As in the passing of this gift
Body and soul are healed.

Let go the struggle where doubt is tied, let go to a Higher Being
Let go and fill each day with hope
Let go, rejoice, and sing.

For each day I rode alone I thought, my cowboy not in sight
Each day I carried him in my heart
A picture oh so bright.

Reality is within our grasp, a fleeting sort of thing
Oh, what a difference this image makes
Pressed into my very heartstrings.

To keep the faith of riding one day, together, side by side
No one can take my Love from me
He's carried deep inside

Today as we struggle to saddle up, I soaked in every pain
So many years have come and gone
Each, preparing this moment of gain

I never let go the possibility of my cowboy by my side
Ever time I had to go it alone
I felt him as my guide.

Never failing to help me whenever I needed him most
Relying on lessons learned I spoke to him in silent words
From my heart, where his image is burned

These conversations seem odd to some,
Not knowing such closeness was there
And yet for me it was common place
Quiet-talk, just like a prayer.

The trail gets narrow and one must lead as single file does form
I see the dust as it billows ahead
He's in front; my faith re-born.

His guiding compass; he knows the way
He has been here many times before
And so I willingly fall in behind
As I witness this open door.

Allowing me to know how it feels, without my cowboy love
Holding tight to an image by faith
Orchestrated by my Creator above.

Never again will I have to ride alone, my cowboy not by my side
For it doesn't matter what reality says
Love is carried deep inside.

God gave my cowboy love to me, so we both were able to grow
Through the trails of life I did discover
A greater gift I'll never know.

Bunny Dryden

*This came after ten years without my husband being able to ride due to a
back injury. We finally were back in the saddle when this was written,
and just a few months after, he had another severe accident rendering
him unable, again, to saddle up and ride. However, healing has occurred
to the point of once again being able to ride together. This is a most
sacred time for us as we ride and listen to only the sound of hoofbeats
and heartbeats.*

Night latch friendship

The kids had quit crying
The dishes were picked up
The dryer was drying
Now coffee in my cup

I tried to call you then
My brief moment today
Voicemail picked up again
Maybe you're feeding hay?

It took a few hours
But you Facebook'd me back
Bottle calf had scours
So you picked up the slack

I saw my phone had chimed
But I was elbow deep
This diaper was ill timed
Hopefully now he'll sleep

Day had turned into night
Before I texted you
Standing under stage light
Had been your current view

You tried me back Monday
But I couldn't be found
The skies had turned dark grey
My cell service was down

By Wednesday I e-mailed
No I hadn't forgot
My husband's help had bailed
I's driving truck a lot

It took a whole week
Before we said hello
Now with the chance to speak
A fit the kids will throw

Our schedules still don't match
We haven't spoken in years
You're there like a night latch
When his head disappears

Thanks for all the friendship
It's been quite the bronc ride
Thanks for taking this trip
Of being a ranch bride

I hope you know I'm here
When your life gets you down
I'm your listening ear
When you think you will drown

Our paths may be detached
But one thing is for sure
As good friends we were matched
Just know that we'll endure

Jessica Hedges

Home coming rain

Thunder in the mountains,
Lord, how we hope it rains.
The pregnant clouds, black and low,
Are held back by mountain chains.

Every day we're watching
Hoping to see them come down
Oh, by the way, we heard it rained,
Up in Prescott town.

Jump over the mountain fences!
Slide down the canyons deep!
Please, dear rain, keep coming,
All the trees begin to weep.

Aha! A bolt of lightning,
Hits the hard dry ground.
And, close! Almost in our house.
The thunder makes it's cannon sound.

We see a trickle of water
Come down the Hassayamp'
It's coming from the north
On down from the Bradshaw camp.

The Hassayampa has been so dry
At least three months or so
It's running muddy water now,
Would you listen to it flow.

We can smell the rain. It's coming!
The air gets hot and still
And soon we hear the raindrops
Fall on the window sill

Another thunder crashes
And all dogs run to the porch
We can smell the Ozone layer,
Where the lightning bolt has scorched.

Coming down in buckets,
We can't see across the yard
Water is running fast, in gushes,
It's really raining hard.

And as we look in each others eyes,
As we, too, sit on the porch,
We see rivers running down our own faces,
That have been so long, sun-scorched.

Carrol Williams

*The Hassayampa River runs through much of Yavapai
and Maricopa County in Arizona. It is often called "Old
Hassayamp."

THE ARIZONA MAN

He was born and died in Texas,
The Lone Star state called home
At the early age of just four years
This cowboy began to roam.

He came to Arizona
In an old Ford touring car.
The roads were a terrible hazard then,
More rock than dirt by far.

He came with father and mother,
Three sisters by his side.
All the way from Texas
To Scottsdale was quite a ride.

He grew up here in the desert.
In the Valley of the Sun.
A tanned and happy boy was he
With time for work and fun.

He learned the things a boy should know:
To shoot and rope and ride,
To plow a field and milk a cow,
Be proud and strong and never hide.

He became an Arizona man,
Straight and true and tall.
With sparkling eyes and dimpled smile
He loved people and critters all.

When war broke out in Europe
And threatened our great land.
He joined the U.S. Army
He knew he must take a stand.

Home from the war this quiet man
Was soon swept off his feet.
By a sweet young gal from Tennessee
This team just can't be beat.

They raised wild cattle,
Good horses he rode.
With a wife and three kids
To help carry the load.

He could quote from the Bible,
Sing the "Cowboys Lament,"
Cuddle a grandbaby,
Ride a bronc 'til it's spent.

Side by side in a cloudy draw
His favorite steeds patiently wait.
To make that last eternal ride
To green pastures through the Pearly Gate.

He will be missed, this Texas boy
With dimpled smile and twinkling eye.
Missed by all who knew the man
For God has taken him home on high.

He was born and died in Texas
This Arizona Man.
Born in the days of the old wild west.
Died with bluebonnets round his van.

*In memory of my Father
E. Wade Allgood
1/19/1920 - 4/16/1993*

*Charlotte Allgood-McCoy

**Charlotte passed away in late May of 2018 just before she was
able to see her poetry on these pages.*

YOU CAN COUNT ON ME

Honey, can I count on you
To be here when the summer's through
And round up plans for fall begin?
"Of course!" I said, "I'll be here then."

Well, August's arrogance wore thin
And as that time of warmth did end
As October's chill came round
Leaving summer spread upon the ground.

Yes, I reluctantly recall
That season's vow, but now it's fall!
And though the air of Autumn's fine
I hate the cold of winter time!

Well, fall's nearly done and now I fear
That roundup's late, *again*, this year.
The air is turning cold and gray.
A winter storm is on its way.

I grain my horse and saddle up
And leave behind my coffee cup.
With boots and chaps and hat bent low
I step outside where north winds blow.

My husband rides off to the east
And sends me to the west.
"Let's make sure this pasture's clean!"
"Okay," I said. "I'll do my best."

Soon fat flakes are lightly falling
And I strive to hear a calling
For me to turn and head toward home.
Guess I'll just ride on . . . alone.

Now the clouds have dropped so low
They've swallowed up the brush below.
I fear they've also swallowed me.
I guess . . . I'm where I'm supposed to be!

There, ahead, is the pasture gate.
Good, that's where he said to wait.
So I pull up and look round
And hope for hoof prints on the ground.

But there is nothing here but me.
I hope I'm where I ought to be!

My horse and I are frozen fast
As hours slip so softly past.
My ears are strained for any sound,
As taunting flakes spin round and round.

Faster, faster they dance and reel
As if my confidence to steal.
I know he told us just to wait,
But does he know our frozen fate?

Briefly, I let my mind go free...
Am *I* lost, or is it *he*?

In this silent, lonesome land
I sit in quandary of our plan
And wonder if I heard him right
As my horse and I turn frosty white!

I think and wonder, should I flee?
Am *I* lost, or is it he?

I see no men or cattle here
In this ghostly atmosphere.
What if they've all gone home
And left me out here all alone!

Suddenly the muffled sound
Of horse's hooves upon the ground
Comes wafting through the frosty air.
I see a shadowed figure there . . .

"You're just where I knew you'd be!"
"Of course," I said, "you can count on *me*!"

Shawn Cameron

119

Neighbors and Friends

Early in the morning
Before the sun comes up
The corrals come alive
With trailers and pickup trucks
Comin' friends who live in town
Or on ranches that are near
They all come out to help a man
Whose friendship they hold dear.

There's an artist, an electrician,
Block-layer, ranchers too!
Each is there to lend a hand
Like thy know this man would do.
They heard he's under the weather
Can't work again 'til fall
His wife and kids his only help
No money to hire it all.

Some folks came out real early
And gathered cattle in
Now the rest have joined the fray
To brand 'em for their friend.
They're settin up the cook fire
Put on a pot to brew
So there'll be some coffee
Set out the biscuits too.

The cows and calves are sorted
Bulls are run outside
The brandin' fire is burnin'
The smoke sure stings their eyes
The cowboys rope and drag the calves
Up close for others to brand
Some are mugging' or givin' shots
They do the best they can.

The smell of stinkin' burnin' hair
Soon fills the morning air
Dust boils around as cows and calves
Are crying, trying to pair.

After all the brandin's done
They mother up the calves
Separate the ones to ship
Count the crop they have.

They take some time to grab a bite
And let the horses blow
Cattle sorta' settle down
'fore they gather 'em up to go
While some are loading cattle
Others take that time
To herd the cows and calves on back
Along the north fence line.

Drive 'em to a water tank
Where they'll find lots of feed
Salt blocks and some cottonseed
Everything they'll need.
Before thy know, the day is gone
And sun is goin' down
They have a satisfied feelin'
As they stop to look around.

At all they have accomplished
In such a pleasured time
And the reason that they did it
Really makes 'em feel fine
You see, that's just the way it is
Out here upon this land
Neighbors help their neighbors
Just like in God's big plan.

This fella doesn't feel ashamed
About his special need
He knows that when he has the chance,
He'll sure return the deed.
And friendship from the likes of these
Who lend a helping hand
Is precious and provision
From his God, as well as man.

Suzi Killman

No Going Back

My childhood home—the deep south
It hasn't fit for years
A beautiful glass slipper
But not my size
I'm kinda like a bonsai tree
Clips have shaped me
Now I grow in odd directions
With so much funny-shaped space
In between

It's not like I'm trying to make it fit, either
But every time I'm back there
For more than two days
I try it on again
Like I might try on an old high school formal
To see if I can even zip the zipper

The Colorado high desert valley I call home
Is my glass slipper
A ballroom where magic doesn't quit at midnight
Where a dream is a wish your heart makes
When you're wide awake.

Peggy Godfrey

The Resumé

It was rainin'
And the weather was gainin'
So I lingered in the house a spell
To avoid the muddy hell
That awaited me outside my door

Cup of coffee by the window
All I can hear is the wind blow
As rain pelts the window pane
True, a lovely, sweet refrain
But it buggers up the chores on this fine morn

I pick up the paper to delay
The starting of another day
Leafing through page by page
Browse advice some call sage
I stop to read the ads-help wanted

Sellin' phones, sellin' cars
Be a waitress at the bar
Front office for the local doc
Or landscaping and moving rock
Then a crazy thought crossed my mind!

What if on some fine day
I had to write a resume
A job in town I'd need to find
Nothing fitting comes to mind
See, I have the skillset of a rancher's wife

Build a fence, ride a horse
And cook some supper up, of course
Brand a calf, doctor a cow
Run the tractor, pull the plow
Heck, I don't even mind the business end of a shovel

Clean the house, pay the bills
Head on out across the hills
Drop some salt at Dillon tank

Prep the papers for the bank
Corral the children that run amok

Patch his wounds, patch his jeans
Help him out by any means
My love and pride I will not hide
As we work side by side
Shoulder to shoulder on this ground we love

So, how would I present myself?
To a desk-jockey seeking help
Yes, I can type and I can file
Greet your customers with a smile
But my heart would not be in it

I think I'll up my prayers to God
We never have to leave this range
I don't want to be displaced
A nine to five to ever face

My skillset is so perfectly geared
To a life that I hold so dear
My hands and body know the tasks
That the duties of each day asks
Uniquely suited to this life and proud to be a rancher's wife

Mary Matli

Hospitality

When I was just a young girl, I loved to play restaurant. I can remember having an old, wood cook-stove as my favorite place to play. It was near our big front porch on the ranch I grew up on near Mayer, Arizona. My kitchen was set up against the backside of our fireplace and was surrounded by huge old locust trees. Not only did those trees provide the walls and canopy of my "place of business," but they also provided long brown pods full of locust beans that I used in most of my menu items. Mud pies by the dozen, skillets, pots and pans full of beans, rock/bean soup, and black bean cookies were always available to anyone that would take the time "order" anything from me!

Little did I know that the Lord was instilling a gift of Hospitality in me at such an early age. I can remember being so excited when my folks bought a real camper that sat on the back of our "town truck" sometimes. I would play for hours in that tiny space that had a "real" stove, sink, refrigerator, and table with benches! I would "cook up" lunches, make concoctions, take orders, and happily do dishes for hours. It was such a thrill when a real live person would come in and let me serve them something!

Later, when I was in high school, two of my favorite jobs (away from the ranch) were stocking shelves with canned goods and grocery items at Downen's Market, but what I really loved was waitressing and making home-made pies at a little cafe down the road. I flew first class to Hawaii one time and thought I wanted to be an airline stewardess so that I could serve the people while traveling all around the country. But that was not to be.

I did take somewhat of a cooking and serving sabbatical during my college years at Sul Ross State University. We were blessed to have a great cafeteria that served a rotating menu of fresh cut pot roasts, steaks, hamburgers, hams, and pork chops from the Meats Lab. The horticulture classes provided many fresh vegetables and the ladies behind the counters could certainly make some mouth watering home-made breads, cinnamon rolls, and tasty desserts. We also learned how to cruise the one way main streets and usually end up at the Alpine, Texas college hotspot of the famous drive-in Sonic. That was not exactly a healthy choice or good for the waistline, but we sure thought it was the "cool" thing to do!

After graduation and learning to live in the big city near Fort Worth, Texas, again I didn't use any culinary or hospitality skills. It was all this country girl could do to survive in a hustle bustle life, and I was working nearly non stop as a Registered Veterinary Assistant "always on call." When I finally got moved back to somewhat quieter, more peaceful Prescott, Arizona, I was living a pretty carefree unwed life and realized that even though I could still make scrambled eggs and quesadillas, drive through fast food and sad to say, too much liquor, nacho cheese Doritos, and peanut M&Ms ended up being the majority of my meals.

I must mention that my mom taught me much better than that! She has always been a great cook, always had excellent hot meals ready for anyone at anytime, and except for the occasional Oreos, she had home-made cookies in the cookie jar. And my dad is no stranger to a kitchen. He is also a great cook, especially good hearty breakfasts. I think cowboys just have an "upper hand" from having to cook whatever was available if they wanted to eat from their early days of "baching" on very rural stretches of land known as western ranches.

As fate would have it, a young cowboy caught my attention. When I finally went to visit him, it was down a very long dirt road that eventually came to a itty-bitty shack of a place known as Halfway House. It was named that because it was nearly halfway to nowhere on that big beautiful ranch in central northern Arizona!

There, my soon-to-be-husband showed me some culinary skills I had never been introduced to. He had one of those built-in flour bins that held about 50# of flour in that tiny kitchen. He tilted open the drawer, put some baking powder, salt and poured canned milk into a little well he made right in the middle of that white, fluffy pile of powders. My eyes were wide with wonder, and when I asked what in the world he was doing, he replied, "making biscuits. This way you use just the right amount of flour and you don't have to wash a bowl." Cowboy Bachelor Logic! And yes, they were mighty tasty. And yes, Louis actually taught me a lot about running a cowboy kitchen in those early years of matrimony!

The definition of hospitality is the act or practice of receiving and entertaining guests, visitors or strangers. That has certainly been a big part of my life. I love to serve folks, and I'm always

126

thankful there have been enough groceries in my various ranch kitchens. Being married for nearly three decades now, I must say that some meals have certainly been more interesting than others. But when you live many miles from the nearest grocery store or even any neighbors to borrow anything from, its amazing what a creative cook can either make-do with, or make-something-up-with-what-you-are-blessed-with from the freezer and abundant pantry shelves!

Feel free to ask me sometime about some of our most memorable meals. Like the supper of tomato soup served in the enamel dog dish, the Thanksgiving bologna and cheese sandwich feast, the invention of beef-enchilada-rice dish that was quickly birthed because Jake the dog enjoyed the hot meal lovingly prepared for the hungry fall cowboy crew before we could make it back to the house from the cattle pens.

Probably one of the all time favorite memories, has to be about roadkill. The freshly weaned youngster sadly spilled from an un-welded trailer gate going down the mountain. We stayed up all night to not waste a single bite of broken backed bovine; cutting steaks, small roasts and hand cranking mounds of veal burger from the little manual cast iron grinder we have. Thankfully, I had enough butcher paper on hand to wrap a freezer-full of milk-fat tenderness. The Lord always provides for our needs.

In the good book of scriptures, I love Colossians 4:5-6. "Be wise in the way you act toward outsiders; make the most of every opportunity. Let your conversation be always full of grace, seasoned with salt." Wherever I may live, if you find yourself close to my kitchen, please stop in! I'd love to sit and chat awhile, listen to some of your stories, create a meal, or even share a snack and a hot cup of coffee with you!

Cindy King

127

BIG BAGS IN THE STOREROOM

One thing a person has to get used to working on ranches is being far enough away from town that trips to the grocery story are few and far between. Buying big bags of staple goods becomes a necessity, not a money saving gimmick.

We spent a year or so in Washington and Oregon with our three little ones where we were a once-a-month get-to-town kind of family.

Gale's mom and dad came to visit, and she being well known for her tasty pies, and Gale's favorite being apricot, she was provided with fresh apricots and went to work. Those pies cooking in the big wood stove smelled mighty good, and browned up perfectly.

When Grandma Monroe took them out of the oven, a little hot juice got on her fingers and she automatically put them in her mouth. She gave a shudder, and said, "That tastes like salt!"

I immediately knew what had happened. Where they lived, in Arizona, they were pretty close to a grocery store. But being far away, we bought supplies in large packages. She had dipped into the five pound bag of salt to sweeten her pies!

Needless to say, she was rather humiliated. And, to add insult to injury, the pies had to be buried so Patty's banty chickens wouldn't get an overdose of salt and die.

Grandma's remark was, "First time I ever had to bury a pie."

* Bertha Monroe

128

A.J.B.

The morning air was cool and clear
As we rode out to help Red
Range brand his early calves
On his Apache Mesa spread.

Fresh horses snorted, hooves rattled rocks,
You could hear our spur rowels ring.
We were seeking out adventure
In whatever the day might bring.

Way out on a grassy flat,
Far from mesas circled 'round,
Was a flagstone marker sticking up,
Set deep into the ground.

As we moved our ponies closer,
The scratching on it could be read,
A.J.B.—etched in the flagstone.
A.J.B.—was all it said.

So we wondered about the story
Behind what had taken place.
But the stone just stood there silent—
A.J.'s fate had left no trace.

Was he running after cattle
And this was where his pony fell?
Or had there been an argument
And life had ended with a shell?

Well, we reined off towards the mesa
For we had cattle to find,
And the challenges we met that day
Drove the gravesite from our minds.

In a country that's hard on leggin's,
We combed the brushy, rocky hillsides.
Four fires later, eleven calves
Carried the *Birdhouse* on their hides.

As we headed in, my thoughts returned
To the marker's mystery,
And I vowed to ask some old-timers
If they knew of A.J.B.

But for now, the secret lies with him,
Buried out there all alone,
Above him only grass and sky
And just initials on his stone.

Kay Kelley Nowell

WHAT IS TOO MUCH WATER?

It was the middle of July, 1962 at the Cross U Ranch. Thunderheads had been building up, rolling over the mesa above the house, and we could see the storm dropping hard rain in the canyons.

Our older kids were used to our admonishments to watch the weather and get back before rain started. But the three youngest daughters, ages eighteen months to four years old, had probably never heard or taken full notice of our words. They had free run of our fenced yard, but frequently found their way over or through the fence to widen the grasp of their playgrounds.

They left our fenced yard to try to find our two oldest, who had gone a mile or so up the road to what was called the "Lodge." The ranch owner brought his four children up every year to stay, and play several weeks in the summer. Between the Lodge and our camp lay a creek bed that was dry except in the rainy season.

Ingersoll, Wallace, and I had just finished doctoring a bunch of steers brought to the corral and gone to the house for coffee and a break. Ingersoll Heckle was a one-eyed old cowboy who would come up from Lakin Milling in Tolleson to help gather steers and check animals for disease before shipping for fattening.

Suddenly, Ingersoll looked up from his coffee cup and sat listening. A rumble had started up the canyon and was growing louder by the second. He jumped up, ran for the screen door, yelling, "Where's them babies?"

Through the gate he ran with Harp following close behind, and me on their tail as hard as I could go. Somehow we just knew where them babies were.

Harp outran Heck, reaching the creek bank just as the second wave of muddy water came into sight. There, in the road to the lodge, in the middle of the creek, were three little girls, water up to their armpits. The oldest was clinging to a salt cedar stem, holding her sister's hand, and the next holding onto the littlest one as tight as she could.

Harp ran into fast-running waters, and by the time he reached those girls, the second wave of water rushed in around them.

Water was up to his knees. He had a little one under each arm, and the oldest had hold of his back pockets as he dragged his way through the mud, debris and rolling rocks. I met him mid-stream and grabbed a baby, and we made it back to shore, barely able to pull ourselves out of the third wave as it tried to pull us all downstream. Two of the little ones had a ring of cedar berries and debris making a perfect halo around the top of their little blond heads. I shivered to think how close they came to becoming "little angels."

Ingersoll was sitting, out of breath, sliding into water, coughing, but he reached out to help me with my load. Looking back, there was my pale husband, struggling with the other two little girls while water swirled up to his belt, tugging them downstream. How they made it to shore is beyond me, but I believe to this day the hand of God boosted him along.

Beyond him were the older two on the far bank trying to get to the kids from the other side of the creek. "Get back!" I yelled to be heard over the rumble of rocks and crash of debris. "Get back!" I don't know if they heard me or saw we'd made it to shore and decided not to try the rumbling creek. But they stayed put.

Believe me, a dry creek can flood in the time it takes to pour a cup of coffee! The canyons in Arizona are steep and rocky, and when it rains hard up there it drags all manner of matter with it. I've seen grown men stuck in a swirling mass of water and debris, unable to outlast the power of fast moving water. Terror strikes at the heart of those who do not heed the warnings. That ... my friends... is when there is too much water.

Roni Harper

Shadows

She watched 'em ride away each day,
The only two loves of her life.
The one she reared, he calls her "Mom,"
To the other she's known as "wife."

Each sat his gelding straight and tall.
She lived to watch 'em rope and ride.
Each dark-eyed, tanned and square shouldered.
Their Stetson hats were worn with pride.

They were shadows in the horizon
As they rode off beyond the crest.
She was feelin' they shouldn't go,
In her bosom, a great unrest.

She told 'em what she was feelin',
They assured her they'd be just fine.
They'd just be checkin' cows and calves,
Mendin' wire on the lower line.

When her cowboys did not return,
Somethin' fragile inside her died.
Now, she sits among the shadows,
Top the horizon, where they ride.

In her mind, she sees 'em leavin'
Just as they did those years before.
Laughin', jokin' and lovin' life,
Waivin' those Stetson hats they wore.

Tho' it's been over forty years,
In her mind, she sees them ridin'.
Behind those vacant, lifeless eyes,
She is somewhere in there, hidin'.

Forty years since they rode away.
Father and son were checkin' stock.
Planned to spend the day together,
Bunchin' cattle with time to talk.

They started out before daybreak,
Mornin' shadows across the crest.
This wife and mother was concerned,
Fearful, told them of her unrest.

They answered they would be just fine,
They'd be checkin' cows, calves and fence.
Soon bein' free to ride their land,
Payin' no mind to arguments.

They waived their Stetson hats good-bye,
Pushed their fresh horses to a lope.
They dogged cows and calves together,
Each snakin' loops out with their rope.

Cattle strayed off down a canyon.
The sides were sandy loose and steep.
Both geldings rolled as ground gave 'way
Into a clay wash, wet and deep.

Father and son lay together
Beneath their horses, in the sand.
Knowin' that their time was nearin',
Died, as son found his father's hand.

After forty years of watchin',
Slowly raises once lifeless eyes.
She smiles as arms and hands stretch out.
She mouths, "I've missed you!" as she cries.

Her cowboys ride off down the crest.
She hears the two loves of her life.
The one she reared, he calls "Hey, Mom!"
The other breathes, "I love you, wife!"

They wave their hats above their heads,
Their dark eyes moist, their shoulders square.
The pounding of the hooves is heard,
Sky shadows cast an eerie flare.

Each prairie night, when work is done,
When sun's settin' and moon's risin',
Look close ... and you'll see her riders,

As shadows in the horizon.

Sam Deleeuw

Desert or woman

The desert is confused as a passive kind of place
One lacking in any real character or design
The unknowing might mistake it as a waste of space
But I know the world that exists below the jack pines

For starters, she is as fierce as she is enchanting
The kind that lets you know you may touch but with respect
She's brought countless men to their knees from lack of planning
Vaulted others to riches they could never expect

Many see an endless pattern of sage-covered hills
Maybe a few rocks or flats thrown in for good measure
But I understand each crest and jag has its own thrills
Each spring, meadow, and cache of ore a revered treasure

She uses fire and rain to tear herself apart
With the confidence to know she can rebuild again
Her rebirth, a tool in a personal kind of art
A rebalance of forages create her new Zen

Some people choose to fear what lies beyond their known world
Frightened by the dance to the beat of an unlike drum
The desert found the groove of the wind as it swirled
Just taking what is to determine her own outcome

Her strength and her history have surpassed the ages
She has met with destruction yet flourished again
A master of life's realities that fill pages
You won't change her but you might get in sync with her spin

Jessica Hedges

GRACEFULLY GREY

She watches her man headed up from the barn
She breathes a big sigh of relief
That silly old fool's been horseback all day
Now he's sneaking back in like a thief
She said, "I've been worried"
He said he was sorry, somehow lost track of time
Like the fifty-three years she's been married to him
Gone by in the blink of an eye

Three babies raised in cabins and camps
A family that God surely blessed
The cover worn thin on the family Bible
By hands that were put to the test
The heart of a saint, a backbone of steel
And a crown she proudly displays
With a satisfied heart from a life well-lived
The lady goes gracefully gray

He reads the *Livestock Weekly* while she's cleaning up
Like all of the evenings before
She thinks how this life is coming full circle
How the kids don't come 'round anymore
But, the grandson is coming to live on the ranch
He's got cowboy blood in his veins
So when the time comes for the circle to close
His hands will take hold of the reins

Three babies raised in cabins and camps
A family that God surely blessed
The cover worn thin on the family Bible
By hands that were put to the test
She pulls out the pins, shakes her hair down
At the end of her "typical" day
The girl in the looking glass isn't all gone
She's going gracefully gray

With a satisfied heart from a life well-lived
The lady goes gracefully gray

Jean Prescott / Randy Huston

RIP TIGGER

The five a.m. sky moved toward five-thirty brightness as I held him cupped in the palms of my hands. He took a breath and then another until there were no more. No, I did not sit up all night. I knew at bedtime that he was too weak to live much longer. I got up around one a.m. to try the thick sticky formula again and refill his hot water bottle. But I slept fine until just before five when he began to cry, almost inaudible sounds coming from the box. Then, I lay in bed, curled on my side, as the day began, and warmed the tiny kitten in my hands as he died.

He just wasn't strong enough—and it is not as dramatic as all of that. He is one of several kittens born in this barn, on this ranch, in this spring. I interfered—and paid my dawn penance.

The mother cat is the mystery. Did she kick him out of the nest, or did she carry him out and place him where we would find him? Did she abandon him as the Plains aborigines did their weak during times of tribal stress, or was she asking us to save him and my efforts were too clumsy?

This is not a tragedy. The life/death/life cycle can be accepted, absorbed . . . and it must be. It is where I live. Sure, my eyes welled with tears as he gasped through those last minutes, hardly any ounces resting in my hands, but there is no comparison to real death and grief. One of my best friends held her son in her arms, her head on his chest—felt and heard his last breaths. He was 26 years old. The stories don't even belong in the same book.

Yesterday the tiny kitten rested in a box with a hot water bottle in the seat of the ranch truck while we saddled up, sorted the shippers off the group of cows in the corrals, unsaddled and put our horses away, and loaded the four steers, two heifers, one old cow, and two bulls to go to the livestock auction. He rode along as we bumped over the rough roads and then smoothed out on the highway. At the sale barn, I stood on the boards of the maze of pens and yelled back and forth with a local cowboy who asked if I had seen my son ride that bronc in Wickenburg and then told me how he knew that kid's day was coming. Then he reined his horse around to start sorting the cattle we brought in, the old cow stumbling along, her service to this ranch unrewarded. We made a stop at the vet's office for kitten formula before buying groceries.

"Life's a dance you learn as you go. Sometimes you lead, sometimes you follow." And sometimes you spend sixteen dollars on baby kitten formula. And sometimes you greet the dawn counting breaths until they are no more.

Amy Hale Auker

*Dedicated to Tigger, of course, who didn't bounce. And to Gail who only rolled his eyes once and understood what was going on as the sun rose and paid for the kitten formula.

THESE THINGS I KNOW FOR CERTAIN

I don't claim to know very much,
but these things I know for certain.
Hymns sound best when sung outdoors,
and old bed sheets make the best curtains.

Coffee tastes best from a percolator,
with canned milk, rich and creamy.
Fresh bread smells like heaven,
sliced thick with butter, hot and steamy.

Sheets feel delicious when dried outside,
they capture the smell of the wind.
While on the line they make a great tent
for kids who are playing pretend.

Lipstick and dresses look good on the ranch,
although practical, they really are not.
Neither are flowers, but yet they still bloom
atop my fridge in a hand-painted pot.

Soft dirt belongs between my toes
when the air warms up in the spring.
Lilacs make the sweetest perfume,
better than a sample in any magazine.

My cheek rests on my husband's chest,
when I lean into his strong embrace.
I can smell dirt and sweat from his work,
and feel his shirt snaps press into my face.

Freedom lies just beyond my front door,
when I step out into God's open country.
No locked gates, crowds or traffic,
just the cactus, cedar trees and me.

Jolyn Young

GRANDMA'S PULLIN' UP DRAG

I've heard it said that the West is dead,
But partner, I hate to brag;
Small saddles with big dreams made a handsome team
With Grandma pullin' up drag.

Cowboy kids love the land, and understand,
When hearts are brave and true.
And the smallest of all will push, scrap, or crawl
To be part of Grandpa's crew.

One slipped a cinch, got dumped, didn't flinch;
Another just had a loose girth.
But the oldest can track and sure bring 'em back,
Showin' how much she's worth.

With hat, spurs, and vest, he's ready for the quest;
The youngest sits ready to roll
He and his cousins are watching as dozens
Of cows call to calves at the waterhole.

Grandmas always worry and tend to hurry
While bringin' up the rear
Keepin' an eye on the little guys
Who are completely absent from fear.

After all, it wasn't so long ago, though,
That Grandma rode the same seat
Ridin' bareback, gathering, flirting with lightning
The challenge was pretty sweet.

Ranch kids today preserve yesterday
They love this land, their cows, the flag
They've got the best of the young ranching West
And Grandma's pullin' up drag.

Sue Jones

Enough

I start every morning with coffee and three written pages
Though I wasn't born to it, disciplined is what I must be
For if you hunger to put pen to paper to draw wages
You've got to pay your dues because
     those accolades don't come free
Someday, I'll be enough.

Next it's on to kids, cooking, the same house chores I did before
I've had it to here with chaos reeked from my toddler boys
Lacking in balance of love and rod for ages three and four
The joy from this season of my life is under dirt and noise
One day, I'll be enough.

I've listened to him vent about a job I cannot control
When words of support or reality only make it worse
He always finds the task that means I didn't fulfill my role
An accomplishment on my part gives him more reason to curse
Maybe, I'll be enough.

Amidst all this failure I find myself behind some black cows
Lazy witches but the work makes me feel needed and happy
One day, I'll be able to cowboy with my heroes I vow
"Just stand strong despite the nay-sayers
     and keep yourself scrappy."
Hoping, I'll be enough.

Every day, lies are shared about this life on stage and on line
Not my job to right them but I can't just sit idly by
While my truth is silenced by lack of makeup and a fake shine
So I'll just keep working, carrying the burden of bad guy
Never will be enough.

Now the search turns inward to finally make myself complete
To look past the noise and the negativity to find me
Being wife, mother, or career woman is no easy feat
Much less the strength and grace it takes
    to carefully balance three
For me, I am enough.

Enough is 100% each and every day at dawn
Enough is the courage to never quit, even when it hurts
Enough is handling stock and people with brains over brawn
Enough is claiming, without shame,
    my place on the high desert
        I've always been enough.

Jessica Hedges

I LOVE FALL THE MOST

The mornings are crisp, afternoons warm and breezy. That's our busy time of year. Heading out to pasture early, checking the mama cows, their babies, and finishing up duties back at the yard. That soft golden glow that settles over the land just as the sun sets, quiet and slow, while cows are talkin' to their babies and them talkin' back.

The flip side is being covered in cattle poo, dirt, more tired than your cow-dog and having four kids needing fed, bathed, and loved on. Moving to the next camp with all you own in the back of a truck and all six of you cramped into the front seat. Scrambling on your knees eight months pregnant trying to tag a newborn calf while mama's snortin' up your flanks.

Cows and horses, whatever other critter you might have around, always needing care and tending. You're never without a bruise, mud, and poo clear up to the eyeballs, and fully vaccinated, dipped, and wormed, totally by accident. Kids workin' sunup to sundown tryin' to make a top hand. All a part of what makes this life seem full to overflowing with danger, mystique, fear, dread, joy, laughter, love, and sharing what most folks never dream of experiencing.

The enjoyment found in the sharing is always worth the hard work. The memories of laughter, love of family, a way of life, the friendships made along the way. Always knowing we were following our heart's cry at God's leading, and He always kept us no matter where our roads led.

Looking back, all I can say is "What A Ride."

Darla Robinson

Pieces of You

The smell of leather greets me
As I open the door
Sweet mem'ries wash over me
And shake me to the core.
I almost hear the cattle
But miss most, my mentor.

Your old Wilson riding boots
Now fit our grandson too
Your son's herd, on our old range
Has grown by quite a few
Everywhere I look these days,
I see pieces of you.

Siblings discuss politics
Intriguing, not prattle
Old stories are told again
Sisters sometimes tattle
My heart hurts each time I see
Cowboys working cattle.

Your brother's hands, shaped and brown
Like yours, I never knew.
Your son stomps his dirty boots
Just like you used to do
Another has THAT smile,
That reminds me of you.

The breeze sweetly reminds me
Of your gentle caress.
The sunshine bright on my face,
The brilliance you possess
Wearing your denim jacket
Brings me comfort, I confess.

Now every time I look at
That ol' Red, White and Blue
Or when your 30-30
Makes another debut
I am so very grateful
For each of these pieces of you.

Lola Chiantaretto

Home

As the sun slips past the hilltops
And the crickets sing their song
Gentle breezes through the hops
Rustle soft and move along
  When the sunlight creeps through billows
  Of clouds so high aloft
  An' sifts down on the corn rows
  Lighting up the corn-silk soft
    Then my heart rests still and quiet
    For it seems I'm home again.

As I watch the limpid dew drop
Slowly move along each leaf
The rustle of the tree tops
And the sparrow's little chirp
  Usher in the distant singing
  Of the piñon in the valley
  And the meadow lark so bold
  As he throws his voice abroad
    And my heart rests still and quiet
    For it seems I'm home again.

The scent of home-made yeast bread
And a pot of pinto beans
A loaf of yellow corn bread
And my faded old blue jeans
  Mean more to me than roses red
  In gardens tended gently
  Than velvet on a silken bed
  Or jewels could ever be.
    For my heart is still and quiet
    Would that I was home again.

When the air is damp, and cooling
And the earth smells warm and sweet
After rain has made a pool
Around the porch here at my feet …

And a butterfly is hiding
In the ivy vines around
Peace and solitude abiding
Gentle nature doth abound
 Then, my heart rests still and quiet
 For it seems I'm home again.

Ah, the world spins faster, faster
Won't it stop and let me off?
Time, truly then a master
Men that stand aside and scoff
 But it only takes a dove song
 In the quiet morning still
 Then my heart breaks forth in song
 Keeps me hopeful then until
  Once again my heart is quiet
  'Til I find I'm home again.

Watching horses, and the cattle
Walk the fence-line on the hill
The windmill softly rattles
At the lonely whippoorwill
 The valley spread below so wide
 The chill of fall night air
 A kitten by the fireside
 And a creaky rockin' chair
  At last my heart is quiet
  For, I find I'm home again.

Sally Harper Bates

A WIDE CIRCLE

A hat, boots, and saddle rest near the altar. Delicate flowers stand in contrast to our memories of the man as we gather to say goodbye to another of the last real cowboys. Our hearts ache for days gone by when these men were tall in the saddle with many good miles still ahead.

Old cowboys should never die. They should just get up one morning, pull on hat and boots, buckle spurs and chaps, saddle up their best mount, call their faithful dog, and ride off over the ridge in search of mavericks. Then when dusk falls and corral stands empty, we could look to twinkling stars and tell ourselves, "He's just makin' a wide circle."

They are rough and tough with lined faces and gnarled, knobby hands. Their hide is brown from the sun and scarred from cat claw and mesquite. Their shoulders and hips wear out from swinging ropes, swinging into the saddle, and swinging more than a time or two around an old dance floor. Their distant gaze scans the horizon – those mountains hold a thousand tales. Memories swirl of days they were larger than life. No horse couldn't be ridden, no wild cow couldn't be caught, and no kid got an easy jaunt.

They come from many walks – some born to it, others drawn to it – all of them embracing peace and quiet in rough country where the only sound may be a horseshoe on granite or hawk wings overhead. And they crave days when the scene was like a Charles Russell painting – wild cow on the end of a rope, horse jerked down, and stampede underway. Ropes would swing. Dust and cussin' would fly. In the end, renegades were roped, bedded, and branded. Then, on tired horses humble supermen would plod back to camp for the night. There, they'd gather around a coffee pot and probably a bottle of whisky, in a warm kitchen, or by crackling campfire, and reminisce in (more than likely) exaggerated detail about the day's events. Laughter and jokes filled the air.

It just ain't right that time sweeps a cowboy away. His rope hangs there on a nail? His saddle waits on the rack? So soon? When did this happen? What day was it that he last stepped down from a cow horse and unbuckled well-worn chaps? Why are his spurs on the wall like relics? Don't they have a job to do?

When God calls him home, we don't question, but our hearts don't understand. We can't adjust the painting in our minds. Despite his gravel-like voice and leathery exterior, he had a heart like honey. We are the lucky ones the cowboy touched with wit, wisdom and Western ways. We can't imagine a day without those spurs jangling toward the kitchen on hardwood.

And so, it kinda helps to tell ourselves . . .

He's just out makin' a wide circle. He rimmed out before daylight to meet Bill, Bob, Fred, Pa, and the rest of the crew. They're saddled up, waiting for him on the other side of the ridge. They have mavericks to catch, and he's one of the best. He's on Sarley, so he's mounted good, and ol' Duke is there to hold 'em up.

If he doesn't get back by dark, we'll light the fire, warm the coffee, and watch the stars begin to twinkle. He's just out makin' a wide circle.

Jeanie Hankins

SPOOKY COOK

The sun was just breakin' in a new day for the cow-camp; Jody was mashin' biscuit dough around the counter, fixin' breakfast for six hungry cowboys. Bacon was fryin' and she'd gathered eggs from the hen house out back, but they were gonna have to be scrambled. The cow dogs between here and there had cold-nosed her and in her jump she'd cracked a few. No big deal—the cowboys didn't much care how the eggs were cooked anyway.

Minutes later, she checked the biscuits and flipped the bacon again, then poured the eggs into a hot pan. She turned to pour coffee as black as mud-daubers into mugs around the table. Three of the boys were knockin' the hay and muck off their boots and reachin' for the screen door. She made sure their cups were full before they hit the table.

About the time she was piling plates full of hot food, the rest of the boys came stompin' in. They seemed to be in unusually good humor. Maybe because they were on the downhill slide for gettin' the fall work done and things were going to slack off a bit before long.

Dave was "primed and cocked" with his usual sadistic humor being bantered about, and nobody was above being his target. This morning, Jody was on the receiving end of more than her share. He dug her about the hardness of her biscuits and pointed out the fact that he'd found a shell in his scrambled eggs ... making a much bigger deal of it than necessary. As they were finishing breakfast, he passed her the butter for her biscuit, and when she reached for it, he quickly raised it just enough to be able to stick her thumb in the soft yellow heap clear up to the first knuckle. She grinned a little cock-eyed grin and wiped the butter off on her apron. It didn't help soothe her feelings when her husband joined in the laughter a little louder than she thought necessary.

They finished and the crew headed for the corrals to saddle up horses that were just finishing grain from their morrals. It didn't take long for those capable boys to be leavin' the camp at a long trot headed for the big pasture behind the house. They'd be bringin' the stock down the fence line after a while, then start sorting bunches in the corrals.

Jody stood and watched the two youngest ones tip their hats to the side and glance back at their shadow. "Little twerps," she thought. "You need a lesson in humility, and I'm pretty sure it won't be long comin'." She knew Mother Nature had her ways of reminding a man just how insignificant he really is in the grand scheme of ranch life.

A couple of hours later she went to pull her dish towels off the line. She noticed the first of the cattle appear over the ridge where the road broke away from the fence line. One of the boys wasn't in the gap where he needed to be, and she could tell those cattle were going to head right down the road instead of the fence line.

"Probably watchin' his shadow again." She grinned as she slipped back into the kitchen and watched the show from her window. Sure enough, once they'd made the curve, there were frustrated cowboys tryin' to get 'em back against the fence so they'd come down the wire and into the big gate to the corrals.

She watched as four men finished the job, moved cattle into the pens, and wondered where the other two were. Missing were young Dave and the other youngster who she was sure were goofing off instead of tending to the drive. They wouldn't last long.

Pulling out a loaf of homemade bread, she began to slice sandwich pieces for an early lunch. They'd be comin' in before they started the sorting, giving cattle a chance to settle. She sliced a roast and stuck a pot of cooked beans on the back burner.

Wiping her hands with a big white dish towel, she glanced out the window to see the two culprits come "packin' the mail" down the road, headed straight for the house. She wondered what was happening; was someone hurt? But the other boys were at the corral loosening their cinches and airin' their horses' backs.

She stepped to the door and watched as the two ignorant young men were showing off in a horse race ... headed right for her back door. They probably thought since it was lunch time, they'd tie up to the hitchin' rail and march right in like they owned the place.

"Well, boys," she thought, "It's time for a little lesson in camp manners." She stepped to the side of the door, leaving it open just enough to be able to slide through at a precise moment.

Just as the boys slid to a stop in the yard, and Dave had his body standing out in his left stirrup to perform a "flying dismount," she opened the door, stepped out, and shook the flour out of her rollin' pin rag with a great deal more flourish than usual.

Both horses snorted and pawed the air as they spun out from under their riders, blowin' snot and hot air clean to the corral, dumping them two young punchers unceremoniously in the dirt near the hitchin' rail. Tails high, stirrups beating them in the ribcage, the horses galloped off with heads in the air, snortin' and blowin' all the way to the barn.

There, they were gathered up by Jody's husband who was craning his neck to see what in the world had happened to set these two horses on the fly with no riders on board. He saw them both rising from the dirt like a couple of Phoenix birds, wings outstretched to beat the dirt off their shirts, straightening themselves up like a couple of errant schoolboys leaving the principal's office. Her husband chuckled and headed for the house.

Jody simply moved back into her kitchen as though what had transpired was as unplanned and natural as it would have been any other time she'd stepped out to shake flour out of the square piece of unbleached muslin. Once inside, she quickly went to the window and peeked around the curtain blowing in the cool mid-morning breeze that wafted in from the snow-capped mountains beyond the borders of the ranch they worked for. She couldn't help but giggle.

She watched as two sheepish young cowboys pulled themselves together and took the reins from her husband. He was laughing by now, poking fun at the joke and joshing the boys a little more than they were comfortable with. They glanced at her front door and pulled their hats down over their eyes as they headed for the corral, still brushing dirt from the seat of their pants.

They didn't come to the house for lunch. She felt some sorry for them and put together a couple of sandwiches wrapped in aluminum foil, sending them to the bunkhouse with her husband when lunch was finished.

They did come in for dinner though. It had been a long, hard day, and they were all tired out, dirty, and hungry. It was sure quiet around the supper table. Extra big bowls of beef stew were dished out carefully with hot cornbread.

When Jody asked for the butter, Dave was careful to be sure she didn't get any on her thumb.

She made hot apple pie for dessert.

Jody Presley & Sally Bates

Sunset

Have you ever watched the shadows
Run across a canyon wall
As the end of day is drawing near
And the sun begins to fall?
The pictures that are etched there
Upon that solid stone
Can only be done by the hand of God
And only His alone.
The colors in the western sky
They sorta' seem to explode
In purples, blues and oranges,
Reds and even gold.
More colors than you can imagine,
Sometimes lined with silver too.
If a mortal man painted such a picture
None would ever think it true.
In this evening time when shadows
Start to reaching out
That's when the critters of the desert
Start to stir about
You might see a while tail deer
Slippin' off down the draw
Or javelina on the ridge
Or a red tailed hawk fly above.
And if you sit real quietly
And listen for the sounds
You may hear the quail a callin'
To others all around.
But if you listen with your heart
For all that you are worth
You'll hear the sound of silence,
So precious here on earth.
You hear your own heart beating,
And thoughts may crowd your mind

Reminding you of a special place
Or a very special time.
You may think of decisions
Made long ago and past
Now, time has told if choices
Were made for good or bad.
A chance to get to know yourself,
You can't hid nothin' here!
You see your virtue and faults
Every confidence and fear.
But bear in mind, you're not alone,
Although you seem to be
Almighty God is here with you
Just like He is with me.
This beauty He's created,
Pictures painted in the sky,
He put there cuz He loves us
Though sometimes we wonder why.
And sometimes things may happen
And it seems so dark and bleak
So God made us a rainbow
For this promise we could keep.
Sometimes when I feel lonely
Don't know which way to go
I walk out in the evening
When the shadows start to show
I watch the sunset in the West
The silver linings too,
And remember with God to guide me
There's nothing I can't do.

Suzi Killman

THE HERITAGE

Four generations ranched this land,
Two are buried here.
Wood and stone still mark the place
They've rested through the years.

Grandpa brought his new bride
A century ago
To homestead on the bottomlands,
Where clear sweet waters flow.

They raised three boys to manhood,
But one went hunting gold,
Another left to serve the Lord,
Just one stayed in the fold.

In time that one son married
A girl named Emily.
They build a home and raised four kids,
And one of them was me.

We grew up knowing cattle
From their bawlin' to their brand,
And dad instilled his rancher's pride
And feelings for the land.

Keep the fences mended,
Give your best, was what he asked.
Never break another's trust
Or let an anger last.

Hard work was just one measure
Of how he judged a man.
If his horse had savvy,
What kind of bulls he ran.

Mama had her own ideas,
But seldom made them known
Her time was mostly occupied
In managing our home.

And I guess we took for granted
Our life out on the range,
But we grew up and they grew old,
And things began to change.

Destiny, it seemed, had plans
That no one could foresee
My sister moved away to teach,
John died at Normandy.

That left Justin and myself
Who made the choice to stay
And we were living on the ranch
When both folks passed away.

Though the world and times keep changing,
The cows still wear *our* brand,
And our kids grew up on horseback,
And learned to love this land.

We're a family grateful for this life,
And what freedom it still allows
Each generation passing on
Its heritage of cows.

Carole Jarvis

GRANDPA'S GARDEN

Newly brought into the family, after marrying their youngest son, never thought too much about cooking, always helped when it was done.

With the scraping and the washing and the putting stuff away, every pan and pot was shining, ready for the coming day.

Countless years these pots delivered meals made with such loving care. Beans, potatoes, squash, and okra, picked fresh from the garden there.

Freshly tilled rows; dark and moist earth, fragrant with that "earthy" scent; waiting seeds were placed along them, Grandpa knew just where they went.

Half a row of yellow crookneck, half a row of zucchini, then the okra, and tomatoes, rows as straight as they could be.

There among the garden veggies, something seemed so out of place. A big bouquet of zinnias, growing in their special place.

This was Grandma's flower garden, mingled with the veggies there, 'cause they wouldn't take much tending, mixed in with the plant life where, Grandpa had to tend his garden, chop the weeds and water too. So there really wasn't any extra work he'd have to do.

Seemed like Grandpa was letting Grandma have her flowers, begrudgingly, but she really had it figured, what a beautiful benefit they would be.

With their fragrance drawing insects to the garden for a meal; burst of color, red, pink, orange . . . bees and butterflies, what a deal!

As they came into the garden, many more than normally would, bees to sample all the flowers, pollinating all they could.

Both the veggies and the zinnias dusted with their magic dust, there was practical and pleasure, side-by-side from dawn to dusk.

Somehow, in this simple setting of a rancher's garden grows, more than just some food for eating, but a way of life that shows just how we can work together, as our differences compliment one another throughout time here as our strengths are willingly lent.

See the beauty of your talents, whether food or flower be, for we are all very special, in the Creator's eyes you see.

Bunny Dryden

SPRING BRANDING

Up on the ridge above the pens,
Now you let your pony blow,
As the bunch that you just gathered
Finds the others down below.

You watch the cattle pour off the hills
And then filter down the draws
Waiting for the rest of the drive
Gives you a chance to pause.

You think back to that early morn
Shared with all the riders there
Dew shone like diamonds in the grass
And excitement tinged the air.

The horses all were feelin' good.
Some forgettin' they were broke
Their riders catching up with friends
Telling lies and telling jokes.

They dropped you off to start your hunt
You covered your country well
Looks like the cowboys got them all
Least as close as you can tell.

Now riders slowly close their net
Like it all had been rehearsed
The cattle funnel through the gate,
Shoving calves that try to nurse.

Those calves get cut off from the cows
And someone makes the tally,
While cows are sprayed and your horse works
To push them down the alley.

And then some hands build up the fire,
Grab dehorners, tags and shots
And sharpen knives as you all wait
For the irons to get hot.

You survey members of your crew
While your horse drinks from the tank,
And if most of them are older—
Chances are—you get to flank!

You tie your horse with loosened cinch
And get ready for the fray,
As ropers start their silent stalk
Of their unsuspecting prey.

Whether they bring them by the heels
Or rope 'em around the neck,
If your flanking partner savvies,
Then you won't get in a wreck.

You both move without thinking
As one is drug out single-hocked
Rope and tail jerk with precision
Like the timing of a clock.

While reaching for that top hind leg,
You hit Mother Earth—kersplat!
A squishy feeling tells you it's
Not bare ground where you just sat.

You admire a stout, loud-marked calf,
Pretty as a spotted pup,
Help puncture, cut and burn his hide,
But pat him when he gets up.

You think back to some other pens
Like where ants got in your pants,
Or when hands got full of stickers
From those Russian thistle plants.

Or the time the calves tore down the fence
And then had to be re-caught.
Well, this pen's in good shape today
But it sure is getting hot.

You've been working hard and steady
Ropers don't give you a break
Your eyes are full of dust and smoke
Almost all your muscles ache.

Seems every time that you get up,
They are draggin' one to you
And there's lots of slick-eared targets
Of the ones still left to do.

You're breathing hard and losing strength,
Fatigue starts to settle in
Then—suddenly—you perk right up
And dash across the pen!

What miracle transformed you so
That you're no longer tired?
You just got told, "Go get your horse
And drag 'em to the fire."

Kay Kelley Nowell

Prairie Burning

Some folks in Kansas City think we should not burn our grass.
They say smoke gives them asthma, which really makes them gasp.
They say it is unethical to produce all that pollution,
So, banning fire on prairie grass would be the best solution.

These folks have the wrong perspective,
They have not thought this out.
Fire is Mother Nature's gift, of that there is no doubt.
When prairie schooners roamed this land, the grass was like a sea
You could look for miles and miles and never find a tree.

The streams and rivers all ran clear as grass roots held soil tight,
Wild life was abundant; native prairie was a wondrous sight.
Then lightning bolts from the sky would set the grass ablaze,
The wild winds blew it far and wide; it burned for many days.

The charred remains were black as coal but soaked up rays of sun
Green grass shoots pushed right on up; a new cycle had begun
The earth was not destroyed as city folks might say
The wildlife thrived as the tall grass grew; it was just another day.

Now, most of the prairie has been plowed to fill our need for food
It has become our fertile bread basket, feeding our growing brood
But out here in the Flint Hills, the grass cannot be plowed,
So native prairie, preserved as ranches, makes us mighty proud.

To prevent invasion of woody plants like cedar, sumac, and hedge,
We must send the fire across the grass, and up each rocky ledge
It does produce some smoke, it's true, but it is not pollution,
It's the by-product of a natural process, which aids in evolution.

We're "sorry," Kansas City, that you must endure some smoke
But we must burn this national treasure, and that is not a joke.
To paraphrase a famous line, your favorite son once wrote down,
"If you can't stand the smoke, then get on out of town."

Betty Burlingham

163

THE GOOD YEARS

The soft sound of hooves on leaves
Shuffling over rock on the slope,
The gentle pull uphill as you look
Praying for grass, praying for hope.

It's autumn and no rain has fallen
No summer monsoons ever came.
Last year's grass is gone to dust
Too many years of the same.

You recall waving gramma grass
Cured brown with seed on the stem
It would put a cow through winter
Up here on the ridge and rim.

But, it rained at least some,
Even those marginal years had grass
The springs and creeks flowed
Laden clouds didn't blow past.

You re-live the really good years
The land was unbelievably green
You rode in mud fixing water gaps
Tanks blown, canyons scoured clean.

Grass and wildflowers were stuff of fairies
Seeds and blooms nodding to dancing dew
Cows and horses sleek and shiny fat
Lord, it was like the land was new.

Those memories keep you hanging on,
Heaven-sent rains would finally come.
You have been in tight spots before
Tough old times, you've seen some.

Drier than the dirty thirties
Record dry they say.
God will open the heavens
Wash this drought clean away.

Till then, you pull your hat down
Squint through the dust some more
Summon faith back in your heart
That God will heal this land's sore.

Close your tired eyes against the dust
See the fat cattle and green grass
Feel the moisture on the soft wind
Dream of the good years of the past.

Deanna Dickinson McCall

His words to her

Pack all your treasures, girl
In the back o' that wagon, girl
We're leaving soon, facing West
Give me your treasures, girl
Trust me with all your world
But come with me . . . facing West.

My world is over there
I do not know just where
But I will always be ... facing West.

Across those Texas plains
Into New Mexico range
And maybe more, facing West
Arizona calls my name
Nothin' ever stays the same
But you'll find me ... facing West

My world is over there
I do not know just where
But I will always be ... facing West

Through heathen savage space
We'll ride to find our place
Somehow we'll win, facing West
You'll have our children there
And find a way to dare
To brave the way ... facing West

My world is over there
I do not know just where
But I will always be ... facing West

Come take a chance with me
Come go where we will see
Wonderful sights . . . facing West.

Through breaks of cedars tall
Pinon and canyon walls
We'll find our way … facing West
Leave all your dreams
Your loved ones dear
Give me your hand and calm your fear.

My world is over there
I do not know just where
But I will always be … facing West.

HER WORDS TO HIM … much later

I packed my treasures dear
Buried all my doubts and fear
And followed you, facing West
You said, "Come follow me
To the land of sweet honey."
We found our way … facing West

Your world was over there
Your dream took us somewhere
I knew you'd always be … facing West.

You promised Northern Lights
We live by lantern light
And the golden glow of morning sun
What was your promised land
Was only barren sand
Your still-born crops, my stillborn sons.

Your world was over there
Your dream took us somewhere
I knew you'd always be … facing West.

You said my Granny's rose
Would grow and flourish there
But drought destroyed every trace

Then came the ice and wind
Freezing rain and blowing snow
Oh, how I came to hate this place.

Your world was over there
Your dream took us somewhere
I knew you'd always be ... facing West.

Now I'm packing up again
Loading what is left of me
I'm moving on, facing West
Tales of gold are calling me
Heaven knows where I will be
I buried you ... facing West

Your dreams were not my dreams
They cost us everything
Your life, and all our sons
Now I'm alone . . .facing West.

Your world was over there
Your dream took us somewhere
Now I must be ... facing West.

Sally Harper Bates

LISTENING TO THEM CHOMP

The summer sun is just a glow as the darkness fades away
I'm strengthened by the renewed hope and promise of a new day.
Closely shrouded by the quiet as I walk out to the pens,
My calling *swo-ook* pierces the air
That's how feeding time begins.
I strain to hear their thundering hooves before they come in sight
They weave their way down through the trees
Like ghosts in the early light.
Ellie swings along there at the front,
As lead mare she's their guide
Sue's hard on her heels with baby, Luna, glued there to her side.
No telling where that Dandy is, off exploring out somewhere,
He checks in just occasionally to nurse his mama mare.
Beside his favorite, Katie, comes the stallion trotting behind,
With an air of calm indiff'rence—bred mares pay him little mind.
Ah, but I remember back in Spring, he fulfilled Nature's call,
Through nuzzling squeals and flashing teeth,
His power was felt by all
With snaking head low to the ground,
He would bunch his little band
Dictating every move they made, he was in complete command.
Behind the barn, the sound of hooves mean it's Foxy and Pooh-bear,
Ambling in from the North Pasture
They, too, come to get their share.
Their demanding, rumbling nickers loudly urge me to use speed,
As I fill grain tubs and hay racks. Each one gets just what they need.
Taking comfort in familiar tools and unconscious routines,
I yearn for answers to just how complicated my life seems.
Here the world can be set right just by providing grain and hay,
And while listening to them chomp, all of my troubles melt away.
Then it's halter lessons, pull out thorns, give someone's feet a trim,
Wipe repellant, dole out fly masks, fill their waters to the brim.
And I envy the simplistic life my "pampered mustangs" lead,
As they leave to graze and play and nap,
Till dusk brings time to feed.

Kay Kelley Nowell

THAT'S WHY!

"But if they ever saw a sunrise on a mountain mornin'
Watched those cotton candy clouds roll by
They'd know why I live beneath these western skies"
– Chris LeDoux

The western life-style is often romanced by writers, singers, stars, and those who quite probably never lived the truth of it. Then, there are those who are privileged enough to actually live it. When I think of the western life style and all that encompasses, from living out of town, to working cattle and managing the land, the very core of me feels whole and complete.

I was two years old when we moved to Wyoming on a ranch near Medicine Bow; it was then that something took root in me. A *longing* to live out, isolated, and the adventure of what that can hold. Something on the inside of me constantly called out to be satisfied.

Fast forward . . . quite a few years. I am married and living just outside of a town in Arizona. I am chatting with a friend about how I would love to move. She said, "Oh, yeah, closer to town?" I replied, "No, farther out. We are too close to town now."

My husband and I decided to make some life changes, and we were able to take a full time ranching job and move onto a ranch located about an hour's drive from town. While this still isn't *way out there,* I can see for miles and miles. It just feels like this is what I was always supposed to be doing.

Everything about the West, from the sky, to the horses, the cattle, wildlife, the diverse topography, to the openness of it, I love it all. Only in the west can you see this great vast amount of un-obstructed views. This, to me, is like someone turning on the oxygen to my soul.

I have had the opportunity to visit the East Coast, and the sky is much different here. I don't know how to explain the feeling of watching a sunrise or sunset, what that does on the inside. But it puts life into perspective for me and reminds me that someone much greater than all of this must be in control, and surely is the very creator of all of it.

Being out and away from the craziness of the city helps me to quiet my soul. It gives me time to think, ponder, and reflect. Reflect on who I am and who I am created to be. What part I play in this world. I don't have the why of it figured out completely, but the solitude helps ground me so that I can better hear the Lord. I want nothing more than to hear His voice and do what He would want me to do.

I am certain He is a cattle rancher, and I believe the West is super special to Him. Doesn't the Word say that He owns the cattle on a thousand hills? Psalm 50:10

That's why . . . that's how . . . the West holds my heart.

Tandy Drye

AT THE RANCH TONIGHT

Snows fall quiet at the ranch tonight
The milk cow softly lows
A coyote trots along a cold ridge
These are the things which my heart knows.

My old saddle horse stands at the gate,
He shakes the frost from his mane.
Ruffled chickens roost in the warm house
I'm not there, yet I know just the same.

My mind sees the deer as they wait by the road,
Poised to leap over the board fence
They bound toward safety down by the creek
Something only my spirit can sense.

As I drive through this rush-hour traffic
And I sway to this city's required dance,
I may be captive within these concrete canyons,
But, my heart's back at home, on the ranch.

Virginia Bennett

Squaw dress

after Dolores Gonzales, *Squaw Dress* c.1940

My own squaw dress was not so elaborate.
If there was a concha belt,
it was nothing like the one you display:

    tooled leather
    intricate silver
    inlaid turquoise.

Memory is hazy but I can picture
fabric one degree toward green
from the brilliant azure sky.

Enveloped in accordion pleats
I take Grandma's hand as she shows me off
at the Rodeo Parade.

    I feel lost.
    I squeeze tight.
    I am seven.

Janet McMillan Rives

THE BUTTON BOX

From the time it was light enough to get outside until way after dark, my brothers and I would be playing cowboys and Indians or chasing an old grey squirrel that lived in the woodpile.

Some days, we would be at the barn, playing with the milk calves or riding our horses. My younger brother and I rarely took time to have Dad saddle our old horses. We rode bareback, and always at a crazy run, as fast as they could go.

One morning, we found Dad and the ranch-hand shoeing some horses they'd brought in from the winter pasture, getting them ready for spring roundup. Trying not to disturb them too much, but being in the usual rush, we asked Dad if he could saddle a couple of them for us. Not wanted to take the time or break his shoeing rhythm, he told us if we wanted to ride we would have to go bareback. I guess we didn't hesitate as I don't remember much after that.

The story goes that we lit out of the corral like those horses' tails were on fire, whipping and spurring as fast as our legs could kick. I was about five, and my brother was a long three year old. We'd pull the horses along side the fence, climb up the other side, and slide into place.

We flew down the old dirt road around by the wood shed and headed to the trail through the ancient orchard. Little did we know that the hired hand had strung a piece of baling wire across the trail and tied a red bandana on it to keep Mom's milk cow from eating any fruit she could reach. Since my horse was in the lead, he saw something he had never seen before and put on the brakes. With nothing between horse hair and old slick blue jeans, I slid over his neck, head first into a pile of rocks.

I had a fractured skull and internal bleeding. My mother said that when they brought me home from the hospital I was confined to total bed rest for six weeks, but for a ranch kid it might as well have been six years. Days drug by, boredom was my bedfellow, as I watched others enjoy what was my past pleasures.

Mercifully, Mom pushed an old brass bed onto the screened

porch, propped me up on pillows, and gave me what had always been known as her box of treasures. Years before marriage and children, an elderly friend of my Grandma had given Mom a black leather suitcase full of buttons. The corners were scuffed, and it had a worn leather handle that had been rewired on one side. The outside of the case smelled musty, like books that had been sitting in an old lady's house, unopened, for years. That smell never stopped me from grabbing the suitcase and pulling it onto my lap.

The minute I would flip the silver fastener open, my world would be transformed. There must have been thousands of buttons in that suitcase! All colors, sizes, and textures. It was like finding a pirate's treasure chest, full of jewels. Sometimes, I would hold the box just right in the sunlight and pretend it was full of diamonds as the light refracted off the surfaces of my collection. Did that one belong to a queen? That one to a soldier who died at war, and his wife kept his buttons for a remembrance? Oh . . . that one . . . must have belonged to a fine lady who dressed in silk and wore a hat adorned with feathers. My favorite were three just alike: surely solid gold surrounded deep green gems that I believed to be emeralds from a far away land. Each button held a story, made up in my mind, and they led me to places far away.

Though I had never heard the term archaeologist, I somehow knew that when I grew up, I would be a "treasure finder." I would go to far away places and find what others had buried forever, thinking to be lost. Perhaps it was the button box that birthed that inkling deep within.

When I was finally allowed to be up and about, Mom gave me a Red Goose shoe box that had been sitting on her closet shelf with sewing supplies in it. She cleaned it out and together we filled it with shards of pottery from the ruins across the road, some pretty pebbles we picked up along the creek, and an occasional arrowhead from Indian ruins we visited that held the history of ancient peoples from our Arizona. Thus, began my life-long passion for collecting.

Cherie Cloudt

THE END – OR THE BEGINNING?

The highlight of our fall months; the shipping trucks rumbling across the cattle-guard half a mile away. Dad was at the scales, he'd already moved shippers into the pen behind the loading chutes, set all the gates, and had his horse saddled and ready.

He'd fed the horses earlier as the sun barely tinted the sky with a glow of daylight. It would get hot this afternoon, but the morning was cool, and a breeze was rustling the leaves in the trees . . . the ones that were starting to turn brown around the edges and curl.

Truckers circled, backed against the loading chute, and left their rigs to shake hands, and then everyone headed for the coffee pot in our kitchen. All gathered around the old oak table with the gigantic claw-shaped feet. Laughter and conversation bounced off the old walls and reverberated in our ears as Mom plopped pancakes and home-made maple syrup in front of everyone. I filled cups and listened intently.

Our early fall works were over. The steers we'd fattened from late February until now on a sixty-seven section permit of high desert Arizona back-country, were leaving us forever. Headed for the feed yard. Thirty days on hot feed and then they would become food for the nation. A high-minded way of looking at the butcher block.

A cup and a refill and then the screen door slammed behind Dad and truckers. My brother followed, pulling his already worn Resistol over his ears, trailing up the caravan, making himself as big as his eight-year-old little person would stretch.

I washed dishes and watched longingly as the sounds and smells of the corral made their way through the open window over the sink. That was nineteen fifty something . . . it was unseemly for a young girl to make her way into the midst of truck-drivers and cowboys. There would be too much cussing, spitting, shoving, and pushing, and Mom was certain I didn't need to be in the thick of things around men we'd never met before.

We stood in the yard later, waving goodbye as two fully loaded double rig trailers made their way up the dirt road. Thirty-seven miles of it were ahead of them, then another hundred and thirty of paved as they made their way to the feed yard. By the time they arrived on the other end, there would probably be cattle down, and the inside of the trailer would reek with the stench of what was left of the feed they'd been consuming the past few days.

It was over. Six months of riding, watching, moving, checking, doctoring, as nearly two hundred head of steers had scattered over the ranch consuming grass and browse. Gaining, growing and maturing. Avoiding the searching mountain lions and rare appearance of a black bear. They'd come to us thin and gaunt. It was late July, they were leaving fat.

Our part was done. Now we would rest a week, go to town for groceries, and maybe visit with friends. Mom and Dad would attend the local saloon and visit with every other cowboy who made his way to town the first of the month. My brothers, three little sisters, and I would take in a movie then play on the grass around the town square until time to head for home before the sun went down. Horses to feed and cows to be milked at the end of that long drive.

The owner of the ranch would be sending a load of bred heifers by the end of August. They'd be scattered over the same high country we'd just cleared, to feed and wander until spring would bring their babies to fruition. *Those were the days of good snow pack and long spring rains. Feed was good, browse was plenty, and grass continued to grow.*

Next spring, works would begin: the gather, branding, shots and earmarks. As long as it was just Dad and us, I'd be allowed to work beside them. I hated when the rancher would send help up from the feed lot . . . it meant housework for me.

The coming year would hold cows and calves instead of steers. A change of pace for us, and an exciting one for us kids. There would be babies on the ground come spring. I could hardly wait.

Tomorrow it would begin again. Dad would ride pastures, check fence, and put out salt. He'd send us to check water tanks and springs. Preparing to receive the young, bred heifers that would carry with them the hope of spring and all those soft faces with curly haired backs. Herefords . . . every one. I could barely contain my longing for days when the manzanita blossoms and wild cliff roses would signal horseback hours again.

Sally Harper Bates

177

Dish soap

The kitchen became my corral
While raising children and foster kids galore
My cowboy experiences were doing dishes
And mopping up the floor.

As I listen to their stories
Of chasing some old wild cow
Or seeing a deer, or lion,
I can visualize it now.

My heart leaps in imagination
As I ride my pony there
And follow the wild mountain trail
Going to who knows where.

I can see those brave young cow-kids
Riding colts, half broke, half wild
And wonder what the city folk
Would think of raising this kind of child.

Children doing men's work,
Trying to make a hand
Taking crazy chances
Just to work this rock hard land.

Now the kids are older
And have children of their own
When the grandkids come to the ranch,
Again it feels like home.

Around my kitchen table
I hear tales like the ones of old
About bucking horses, chasing cows,
And some that can't be told.

As I hear their happy laughter
See the stars shining in their eyes,
I feel a little younger,
And think, how fast time flies.

Carrol Williams

To My Way of Thinkin'

To my way of thinkin' nothin' looks much better
Than the first green breakin' thru the earth in Spring
Or the welcome sight of summer thunderstorms
With the prospect for rain they might bring.

And to my way of thinkin' livin' comes easier
Where the quiet of a winter night is deep
Interrupted only by an owl's lonesome hooting,
And a whispering wind that's lullin' me to sleep.

And sometimes at night with the velvet sky awash,
And a million trillion stars above my head
I can't keep from thinkin' of cowboys gone before me
Who watched this same night sky from their bed.

Sleepin' on the ground, where nothin' veiled their view
Of the heavens that stretched far beyond their sight.
Did they wonder at the splendor there above them,
As they drifted off to sleep in that dark night?

Chances are, their thoughts and mine were much the same
Though decades separate our time on earth
For the cowboy life is one that never changes,
If you're talkin' things of intrinsic worth.

Like watchin' the seasons of the year come and go
Carin' for cattle, just a good horse and you.
To my way of thinkin' life couldn't get no better
But then, that's just a cowboy's point of view.

Carole Jarvis

Times are Changing in the West

Several years ago my sheep shearer told me a story that I cannot forget. In southeastern Colorado there lived an elderly couple who had spent their lives ranching. Though no longer engaged in full-time ranching, they retained a small flock of forty Suffolk ewes.

Escaping the confines of city living, new folks were purchasing land, building homes and moving to the country. One of these new immigrant families had two large dogs, Rhodesian Reds, which were seen from time to time roaming the countryside. Rhodesian Reds are used for lion hunting, and large roaming dogs are known for getting into livestock. They may chase, chew on, or kill stock. Many ranchers simply shoot dogs that come onto their property rather than wait until a disaster.

After seeing the dogs on their property, the elderly couple contacted the new neighbors and asked them nicely to please keep their dogs at home, explaining that no damage had been done, but the potential was ominous. The new folks stated clearly that they had moved to the country so their dogs would have the freedom to run and play.

Some time later, before leaving for town, the elderly couple corralled their ewes who were close to lambing. During their absence the two large dogs got into the corral. Upon returning, they found the dogs amidst the death and dying of their entire flock of pregnant ewes.

Within a couple of months, the elderly man died; soon after that his wife died. Hearts can only contain so much sorrow.

Peggy Godfrey

Pretty Words upon the Page

It is hard to explain some days with pretty words upon the page. The hiss of the flame under the coffee pot at 3:30 followed by the slam of the door on the tin barn. The sound of Ivan, patriarch of the remuda, as he welcomes breakfast, even at this hour. The smell of bacon and the glow of headlamp. Trotting out in the cold early morning in the desert, fingers frozen even though it is May. The aggravation of tying a coat on behind when the day heats up. Gathering cattle from 29 square miles of country, rough country. This week, we are going to the hidden hard-to-reach pockets to dig out the left-behinds, the remnant. It is 7a.m. before we see cows. He stretches his arm out as the sun lights up the opposite side of the canyon. They are climbing out into that sun, welcoming the warmth just as I do. We step off and air our horses' backs, lifting our saddles high to brush out any sticks or juniper berries that have collected there. I can see the cows now. A pretty good handful.

It takes us two hours to get across the canyon. Some of the time we are off our horses, leading over the roughest ground. These mounts must stand up under us all day long. A tired horse is what will get you hurt.

When we hit the cows, we sit with them, peer down the slope, and discuss the best way to get off of here through the rocks and the cactus and the scree. Everything in this low country has stickers or stings. A bee rests in each yellow cactus blossom, but only for those who can see. After a few false starts, the cows show us the way they like to go, and we follow them, though it means later, bending them back around. By noon, the day has heated up, and when we point the group up the trail on the other side, the final cow in line turns her head and bawls at me in protest. Don't I know that any self-respecting bovine is napping in the shade in midday? Not climbing out a steep trail in the hot sun? People think horses are smarter than cows, but I disagree.

A cow's whole life is organized around caring for her baby. She sleeps up on the ridges where the sun will warm her back early while the dim shadowy bottoms remain cold. She stretches and nurses her calf. And eats. She grazes her way perpendicular to the slope, always taking the easy path, moving slowly. By mid-morning, she and her closest friends have gotten to the salt ground and by noon they've hit the water hole where they meet up with a few more friends to nap in the dense overhang of bank or brush or trees. The babies nurse after the long somnambulant naptime, and then slowly, gradually, the whole community grazes its way back up the slopes as the evening sun creeps with them, and they bed down in the final warm rays. It is a good life. My horse, on the other hand, heard the bang and clang of gates at 3:30 a.m. and he must carry me all day, his free will subdued by saddle and bridle and the work that we do.

We hold up on the salt ground, all of us, horses, cows, and cowboys exhausted by the steep white bright straight-up climb out of the canyon with questionable footing in the deep powdery dirt and rolling rock. As I pull cactus spines from my hand and a few more out of my horse's legs, my husband, Gail, points to a heifer with her first calf. She is a very small cow, just now two years old. "I didn't think I'd see her again after John and I put her off in here. She was so heavy. I didn't think she'd make it." I wasn't here on that day because I was back at headquarters tending to a sick horse. I don't often resent getting a series of days off, but I do resent missing out on our shared story. It will take us six hours to get from here to the upper horse pasture at Willow Springs where we saddled up. It is a long slow hot march, single-file, and I have plenty of time to think about shared stories and this little heifer, no longer a heifer, but a cow, tending her young one, a fine and healthy calf, walking like a good soldier up the trail. I am glad she survived a too-early pregnancy. I am glad I got in on the story.

I am in my late 40s, a grandmother, a published author with multiple books under my belt. I could have drunk my coffee this morning from my favorite mug, doctored it with crisp cold half-and-half from the humming refrigerator. I could have sat and watched the birds at the feeder while I put pretty words upon the page. But instead I drank my coffee from a tin cup with a dollop of canned Carnation opened two days ago. I woke two hours before birdsong, because without these days, this shared story, my words are only pretty, just pretty, qualified pretty shallow. They are pretty without the grit that makes them fertile and rich. Or so I tell myself when the day is hard, and I wonder why I don't work at Starbucks instead.

We put these cows through the gate just as dusk begins to settle over the camp in a cool blanket. We've been in the saddle thirteen hours now. I notice that the young cow has bedded her calf down right beside the hay trailer where she will sleep overnight. No more walking.

The trailer gate slams as I enter the barn to get hay for the horses. I enter slowly. A few years ago, being my father's daughter, I entered at a full rush when Gail said, "Let's reward these girls for coming with us." My father's favorite order was, "Trot up every chance you get!" and no matter how many birthdays I have, it is my father's words that will echo in my ears. But on that day, I trotted full-tilt into the barn and grabbed at the strings of a bale only to have a rattlesnake buzz beside my right boot. I ran over Gail on my way out the door. So now I walk slowly into the gloom and peer around carefully before pulling out my knife to cut the strings. No more trotting up, at least in the hay barn at Willow where my name is carved on the old wooden cabinet beside the door. So many cowboys have carved their names and the dates of their time on this ranch. *Amy 2008.* So far, mine is the only feminine name.

It is almost full on dark by the time the door of the cabin slams behind us. At least at this camp we sleep in a bed with a roof over our heads rather than in a bedroll beneath the stars. I stare blankly at the pots and pans and cans. I am too tired to want to cook, or even eat. There is no more whisky ice in the cooler. We will not play a hand of cribbage, and the guitar hangs silent on the wall tonight.

I'd like to end here, say that I tried to explain a hard day, but we go again tomorrow.

The hiss of the flame under the coffee pot at 3:30 is followed by the slam of the door on the tin barn. The sound of Ivan as he welcomes breakfast. The smell of bacon and the glow of headlamp. Riding out in the cold early morning, fingers frozen. Another day in May.

We are not going as far today, but in mid-morning we hit cattle that haven't seen us in some time. We sit quietly at a dirt tank as they settle, become accustomed to our presence. The

Southwest is locked in a pretty serious drought, and it colors everything we do. The land is fragile and easily crumbled, hurting. Only an up close and personal view shows how much it is hurting. From a distance it is very pretty country. We need to get these cows out of here, out of this hot low country and up to a higher elevation. Gail rides around the dam, and we talk in soft voices. "We could run that little long-eared heifer off if we aren't careful. And that maverick bull is interested in that bulling cow, but if he runs off, no heroics. Act like we don't care. Hold what we've got." About that time, three new pairs come over the dam to water. One of the cows has a calf that can't be forty-eight hours old. He's all legs and ears, almost boneless and soft, still wobbling on his tiny hooves. He reminds me of a jackrabbit. The other two calves aren't much bigger. It is six miles, almost all uphill, to camp, but earlier that morning we saw both a lion track and the biggest bear track I've ever seen. These little guys have to go with us, not only today, but tomorrow, another four miles to the corral where we will brand and sort and haul shippers to the sale. When we open the gate, turn them loose, they will have to walk another two miles to water up on the mesa where they will spend the next couple of months. It is a hard life for babies in these mountains. We won't brand the tiniest. We'll get them another time.

Today we take it slow. Like Gail says when we leave the tank in late morning, "Let's just peck along. We have all day." In early afternoon, we hold up at another tank, this one bone dry, and we stay long enough for the calves to nurse while we air our horses' backs. In a good year, everyone would get a drink and a nap in the shade.

We are praying for heavy, healing monsoons. We've had enough of these pretty blue skies.

The rest of the trail is straight up, rough. I'm careful to keep my calf count in view, getting off my horse a dozen times to get the babies back on their feet when they step off the steep trail to collapse in a heap of fatigue in the shade of a bush. The smallest red bull calf on his spindly legs struggles valiantly to keep up with his mother. She bawls back over her shoulder when he lags.

I've been working in this country for ten years. I've been in this relationship the same amount of time. We are two very complicated human beings doing a hard job in hard country. Plus, like everyone else, we have the normal stressors of chores and family and finances and calendars. I don't swing gracefully down out of the saddle when we close the gate behind the cows. There is no cowboy glamor around here, no slim waisted jeans or bling on my shirt. I haven't had a shower in six days, and my hair has mostly been under a hat. I slide heavily to the ground. Our normal is work and horse sweat and dirty fingernails and a whole batch of chores still to be done. But we are at camp earlier than we were yesterday, and so we sit in the evening light with a cool-ish beer. I mention that tiniest baby calf. Gail turns to me with tears in his eyes. "He's a tough little sucker!"

Once again, I stare with blank fatigue at the pots and pans and cans. There are so many words upon the page about a job and a lifestyle in which very few materially or physically participate. There are words and songs of memory and nostalgia, of pleasure rides and wide-open skies, of an ideal that is rarely ideal when experienced. Tonight, the pretty words I know will go onto the page are not about western sunsets, though I am sure I am missing something spectacular. They aren't about riding out into the soul-healing day. They aren't about a good horse between my knees or some elusive ethic or moral or prayer surrounding agriculture.

It is hard to explain some days with pretty words upon the page. Tonight my pretty words are about a man with work-worn hands, about falling in love all over again, about resilience, about a fragile newborn bull calf who walked six miles and the reminder that he is, indeed, "a tough little sucker."

Amy Hale Auker

THE VOICES ...

MARY ABBOTT   It's always been about the horses, the cattle, and the great cowboys she's worked with through the years. Mary is well versed in the ways of all three. She's ridden many a back trail working cattle through some of the roughest country the West has to offer. She and Neil were employed by Maughn Ranches for several years before they retired and moved to Rodeo, N.M. Neil passed in 2018, but she continues to day work for local ranchers in the rough country near Rodeo. Her poetry s always about the life and the memories of many years in the saddle following cattle up some rocky, brushed up trail.

AMY HALE AUKER   Amy writes and thrives on a ranch in Arizona where she is having a love affair with rock, mountains, piñon and juniper forests, the weather, and her songwriter husband who is also foreman of the ranch. She guides her readers to a place where the bats fly, lizards do pushups on the rocks, bears leave barefoot prints in the dirt. Where hummingbirds do rain dances in August, spiders weave for their food, and poetry is in the chrysalis and the cocoon. She tells stories about the real world where things grow up out of the ground, where the miracle of life happens over and over and over again, where people can and do survive without malls or Arby's. Amy believes that what you put out there is what you get back, and that if you do the good, hard work you will be rewarded. Come, visit the world she lives in.

SALLY HARPER BATES   Born in Prescott, Arizona, she never lived far from the manzanita and malapias of Yavapai County. She grew up and worked on ranches in the shadow of Camp Wood Mountain, and she's stayed in the company of the working cowboy element, which has given her good fodder for her stories, poetry and songs. She found the idea for this book birthed with a single thought, a title, and the picture for the cover. Here it is ... *what a ride!* She and her husband of nearly forty years live in Chino Valley, she's mother of two beautiful daughters, their husbands, four granddaughters, and two great-grandsons.

VALERIE BEARD   Born in Yuma, Colorado, out on the eastern plains, she was raised in Loveland, in the foothills of the Front Range. She's lived in Colorado her entire life. While she's always loved to write, she hadn't done much until she and her poet husband, Floyd, began visiting cowboy poetry gatherings. She began putting things down and has recently been an invited poet in her own right. They have two grown children, both married and working on ranches, and twin granddaughters that are six years old.

VIRGINIA BENNETT   Virginia Bennett worked on western ranches in several different states, alongside her cowboy husband, Pete, for 35 years until a work-related horse wreck put the whoa on her cowboy activities. She most enjoyed working with horses and cattle and made a career of starting colts and making good ranch horses for herself and the public. She also drove draft horse teams, along with all the other usual ranch chores. Virginia homeschooled their son, Jesse, for 11 years, up until his graduation. The Academy of Western Artists awarded her the title of Cowgirl Poet of the Year in 2014. Featured at the National Cowboy Poetry Gathering in Elko, NV for 14 years, she and Pete now enjoy living in south-central Washington, where they explore the trails and back roads of their scenic country in their trusty red Jeep.

SEQUENT BODINE   Sequent raised two boys and a daughter in the dirt and dust of rodeo life. Her then husband was a stock contractor for several years in southern Arizona, so travels and contacts with the culture of the American rodeo cowboy was a way of life for her then. They worked on a few ranches and became better acquainted with the working cowboy realm of existence, and that's where the stories she's sharing here were birthed. She currently lives in Surprise, Arizona where she works for Fry's food stores and enjoys her children and grandchildren. As a Christian woman, she says one of the things she enjoys most about her job is that it gives her all manner of opportunities to pray for and with people she meets on the job.

BETTY BURLINGHAM   She is inspired by the abundant plant life, wildlife, gorgeous vistas and wonderful people of the Kansas Flynt Hills tall grass prairie region. After ranching full time for twenty-two years in East Carolina while her husband Byron taught medical school, they purchased an overgrazed and long neglected "retirement ranch" on the Kansas River near Manhattan. They custom graze and work each day to restore the land to productive prairie. She enjoys sharing her poetry with diverse audiences. She's Mom to three amazing adult children and their families.

SHAWN CAMERON   Shawn's poetry and artwork reflect the ranch life she's lived all her life. Her ancestors traveled the Oregon Trail in an ox-drawn covered wagon, then drove 200 head of cattle south into Arizona. She and her husband, Dean, are continuing   a ranching legacy that runs deeply into the sixth generation. She received a B.A. degree in Education and Written Expression from Prescott College, and continued her art through independent study and workshops. She is a professional artist who participates in national museum art shows and is represented by Trailside Gallery in Jackson Hole, WY. Most of her family, including grandchildren, still ranch in northern and central Arizona.

LOLA CHIANTARETTO   She signed on for a crash course in Cowboy-101 at the age of 38 when she married a cowboy who had never done anything but cowboy from the time he was a child. She quickly found herself with many opportunities to develop and refine her own cowboy skills as she worked side by side with Harry. At one point, they were horseback an average of 300 days a year. She began writing poems about the life, love and experiences and her first book was published in 2009. As an invited poet, she presented her work at the Prescott Gathering for several years. Health issues necessitated change, and in 2017 she began a new journey. At the loss of her husband, Harry, she is learning to walk alone again.

CHERIE CLOUDT   She grew up on ranches in Arizona during the 1950s and 1960s. "It was a time in my life that held the sweetest memories and the best stories." After 60+ years traveling the world, living in eight states and a foreign country, she still believes the best times of her life were growing up on ranches. "My love of the ranching culture led me to a MA in Anthropology, studying ranch women and early pioneer women of the southwest." She now lives on the southern Oregon coast, where she spends time researching, writing, and painting.

JIMINELL COOK   Born and raised in Prescott, Arizona, she's lived on and worked for the Cross U, Yolo, O RO, Pipeline, Bar Heart, and Red Rock Ranches. Benedict Feed Yard, Silver State Ranches, Mike Oden Cattle Co., and the 7L Cattle Co. She was co-secretary for the Arizona Cowpunchers Association and Secretary for the Panhandle Cutting Horse Association. As a teenager she was a second attendant Rodeo Queen for the Prescott Frontier Days Rodeo. She's raised five kids and has ten grandchildren so far.

TERRY CROWLEY   Her roots run deep in Arizona cow-country with grandparents homesteading in southern Arizona. The other branch of her family tree ranched near Strawberry, Arizona. Her parents bought the Music Mountain Ranch near Peach Springs, which is where she and her husband Dan are currently ranching. She's lived from Red Rock to Hawaii, Canada and back to Arizona raising five children, cooking for ranch crews and carrying her camera everywhere. Lots of 4H meetings, Bible studies, Sunday School teaching, and a love for the life they were living. Kids all grown now, she and Dan carry on the generational traditions living on the Music Mountain Ranch, raising cattle, and living what most of us would consider a pretty tough life.

SAM DELEEUW Make no mistake, Sam DeLeeuw knows what she's talking about. She has been a part of the agricultural life since she was born. She's raised and herded cows, sheep, horses and two rodeo queen daughters. In college, she was often the only girl in the ag-curriculum and was a popular date because she'd help with the branding and such. Sam's background gives her all the ideas for her often humorous, but sometimes tear-evoking stories. Four-time Female Poet of the Year for the IWMA, Humorist of the Year for the AWA, and 2017 IWMA Poetry Book of the Year. Her most treasured rewards are the people she's met over the years. Raised in Blackfoot, Idaho, she now makes her home in Roy, Utah, and is in demand as poet, humorist, emcee and lively entertainer.

DAISY DILLARD Born in Mimbres, New Mexico, most of her growing up years saw no electricity, no indoor plumbing, and the little outhouse sat non-descript in back. She married her cowboy at age 17, he was 19. They had been married 65 years at his passing. They had two ranch-raised kids, have 9 grandchildren, 24 great grandchildren and one great-great. They bought a small ranch outside of Kingman, Arizona and were there a little over 20 years. Her husband and other cowboys and friends have been all of the inspiration for her poetry. A published poet, she currently lives in Camp Verde, AZ.

JODY DRAKE Lives in Prescott, AZ where she was born and raised in a large family involved in mining, ranching, and the Drake flagstone quarries. She's written and produced twenty two historical plays, portrayed Sharlot Hall in Arizona, California, New Mexico, Texas and Utah. Jody is an Arizona Speaks presenter, an Arizona culture Keeper, nominated for the Governors Arts Award eight times, recognized as a Soroptimist Woman of Distinction. Drake is founding director of Blue Rose Theater. Her personal honors include performing for Sandra Day O'Conner, ex-Supreme Court Judge; ex-Governors Janet Napolitano, Jane Hull and Janet Brewer; as well as Polly Rosenbaum, Raul Castro and many more.

BUNNY DRYDEN   She's no stranger to ranch life, and rides with her husband Newell to gather cattle, check fences, haul water, shoe horses, check pipe lines, brand, doctor livestock (bloated calves, still births, prolapsed cows, mastitis, dehorning, vaccinating, float teeth, remove caner eye, cut bulls, etc.) A closet poet until later years, she is now recipient of numerous awards and recognition as the lead organizer of the Gila Valley County Poetry Gathering in Safford. She lives in Thatcher, and continues her never-ending education as a rancher's wife and writer.

TANDY DRYE   Born and raised in Flagstaff, Tandy planted her roots deep in the piñon and pine country. She and her husband Dale have been married almost 25 years, and raised two children in the environment of the working cowboy. They spent much of their lives working on his family ranch, where he represented the fourth generation of livestock men. They lived and worked there until the ranch sold recently, but put in a stint in Colorado for seven years on another ranch with the other fork of the family tree. They now work on the Walking Cane Ranch near Winona, where they pastor a cowboy church, keep growing beef, and teach their children to respect and enjoy the cowboy way of life.

SUSAN GAHR   Spent a great deal life working on ranches in AZ, CA & Pecos, TX, living on cowcamps and working on several well-known ranches. She rode colts, with help from her brother in law, Twister Heller of Arizona, spent hours riding drag and helping the little ones along, rode with some "pincurl crews" and today rides and helps her husband working cattle. Now settled in Dickens County, TX, she focuses on her art projects. "I love to paint cattle, horses, kids and colts ... from the long-haired little cowgirls to branding crews and shipping pens. A self taught artist for the most part, I just kinda fell into it. Guess if you want to do something bad enough, the opportunities will arise." Susan and her husband, John, help with their local church and their lives have been full of helping other people find their full potential as well. They have three grown boys and a "pocket full of grandkids."

PEGGY GODFREY   Peggy has ranched in the upper reaches of the Rio Grande watershed for forty-four years; the last thirty of those in Colorado's San Luis Valley. Her family consists of "all my blood relatives, my soul-kin, ranchers, poets, and friends." She's been included in numerous poetry gatherings throughout the states, and as for why she loves the West? "If you can tell me why ripe peaches and strawberries are so irresistible, enchanting, I'll attempt to tell you why I love the West."

AUDREY HANKINS   From the hottest desert places in Arizona, to the high country of Colorado, Audrey has gleaned her knowledge of cow-country, horses, cattle and kids. That knowledge, and her gift of putting words on paper has won her numerous awards as a poet and writer. But they don't hold a candle to her "awards" and the battle scars she's "won" in horse wrecks and life in general. A sought after poet for many years, fine entertainer, great mom and all around good help in a corral.

JEANIE HANKINS   Jeanie Hankins was born and raised in the Wickenburg, Ariz., area. Her early years were spent riding with round-up crews in rough desert country, and helping with her parents' outfitting business in the San Juan Mountains of Colorado. She has a bachelor of arts in communications/journalism from Grand Canyon University. Jeanie lived in eastern Wyoming for 20 years before returning to her hometown, where she continues her 24-year community journalism career as Publisher of the Wickenburg Sun. Jeanie has won numerous writing and photography awards from the Wyoming Press Association, Arizona Newspaper Association and the National Newspaper Association.

RONI HARPER   Born in California, her family moved to Flagstaff when she was quite young. She grew up in a family of seven, dependent upon their single mother. A young divorcé at the age of thirty-two, she married a handsome young cowboy and lived in the shadow of Camp Wood Mountain for nearly twenty years. She raised five kids in the culture and community of the working cowboy. When he passed, she gave it all up, moved to town, and raised her youngest children outside of what they loved and lived ... but she carried it with her in her heart, as did each of them. Her writing is full of the hardships and laughter of those wonderful years.

JESSICA HEDGES   She's a wife, mother, cowboy, writer, photographer, and business owner in the high desert of southeast Oregon. She specializes in multi-media presentations of her stories while teaching others to do the same. Branded In Ink keeps her busy, let alone her family and working with her husband where cattle and horses are thick. Her most recent award is the coveted 2016 Georgie Sicking Award presented by the Western Music Association. Georgie was one of the most beloved and respected of cowboy poets, and it appears Jessica is well on her way to following in her footsteps ... just a little ways back.

SANDY HELLER   Sandy lives just north of Congress, Arizona with her horse-trainer/rancher husband Twister and their son Jud. They have two older daughters in Texas and Georgia. "What I truly love about the West is: We still wave to others as we pass on the road, stop to check on folks stalled on their way, and check on the neighbors to be sure they're okay. I have a gentle gelding who takes good care of me, we ride, gather cattle, and enjoy the freedom away from the noise and pestilence so frequently found on the streets of big cities." Sandy and Twister have worked on several ranches in Arizona, but settled into the business of training horses many years ago. "I'm blessed the Good Lord gave me this life, I have some wonderful memories, and enjoy fully the culture and traditions we find in our lives."

YVONNE HOLLENBECK   Ranch-wife, poet, quilter, and in this case songwriter. The words to the poem in this publication were co-written with Jean Prescott, and made their way to the vocal production on one of Jean's CDs. Yvonne is a sought after performer at Cowboy Poetry Gatherings nation-wide, but her rancher husband knows she's just a call away when he needs help on their ranch in South Dakota.

CAROLE JARVIS   Her cowboy/ranch life didn't begin until at the age of 22, when she met a handsome Jackson Hole, WY cowboy. After a summer of courtship, they married and began their tour of duty on several ranches from Oregon to Arizona until time and age caught up with them. Dan passed in 2010 and she's kept a hold on the reins and remained on the last home-place outside of Wickenburg Arizona. Her cowboy poetry has always been a source of gratification to her, a way to share the love she feels for the West and the cowboy way of life.

RANDI JOHNSON   Great Basin native, Randi grew up on cattle ranches in Nevada, California, and Oregon. The experiences she's had with her brothers and the stories that old cowboys tell serve as the inspiration for her poetry. She has a Facebook page called "The Cowboy's Daughter" where you'll find many more poems and stories as well as photos of her family and ranch life.

SUE JONES   She grew up in the White Mountains of Arizona riding horses with kids whose ancestors were pioneers. The western lifestyle was what she wanted, and what she found there. She and her cowboy husband, Bill, live in Rimrock, AZ currently. They've encountered many adventures, both on their own spread and helping friends who are long time area ranchers. Her love of the West is reflected in her poetry which shares her many experiences, frequently with a humorous twist.

SUZI KILLMAN   Raised on a ranch between Prescott and Wickenburg, Suzi grew up riding with and helping her dad where she developed a love for ranching and the western lifestyle. When he passed in 1965, the family moved to "town," but Suzi's heart stayed right there outside! She still loves to work with horses and cattle, team ropes with her husband, Bill, and belongs to a group of horseback women called, "Las Damas" She's a singer and songwriter as well as an excellent poet, has several books and recordings to her credit, as well as the Gail I. Gardner award from the Arizona Cowboy Poets Gathering. She has three children, eleven grandkids, and eleven great-grands. She and her husband have recently returned to manage the ranch she was raised on along the Hassayampa River.

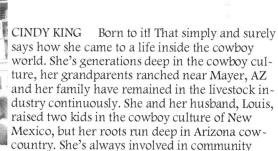

CINDY KING   Born to it! That simply and surely says how she came to a life inside the cowboy world. She's generations deep in the cowboy culture, her grandparents ranched near Mayer, AZ and her family have remained in the livestock industry continuously. She and her husband, Louis, raised two kids in the cowboy culture of New Mexico, but her roots run deep in Arizona cow-country. She's always involved in community helps, church events, and the lives of those who enjoy the lifestyle of the working cowboy and ranching community.

MARY MATLI   Raised on the family ranch in Williamson Valley, near Prescott, AZ, Mary spent several years working in offices and raising her daughters. However, she never let go of her roots and a few years ago walked away from the office environment and went back to work on ranches in Northern Arizona. She is currently holding down the camp at Pipeline Ranch near Congress where she does everything any cowboy would be asked to do and then some. She's lovin' the life and livin' her dream again. An award winning poet and writer, she continues to pour out her dreams and her heart as she walks through every day doing what she loves most. Bein' a cowboy!

197

DEANNA DICKINSON MCCALL Deanna has cows, horses and a love of the land bred into her, coming from a family that began ranching in Texas in the 1840s. She has ranched in several western states, including 22 years raising her family on a remote Nevada ranch without phones or electricity. She now ranches with her husband in the Sacramento Mountains of New Mexico. Her writing and performances have won numerous awards: The Will Rogers Medallion Award, the Georgie Sicking Award, NM/AZ Book Awards, Women Writing the West, Western Music Assoc., The Academy of Western Artists, and the Heritage Award from the Texas Poets Gathering in Alpine

CHARLOTTE ALLGOOD MCCOY Her past is full of horse tracks and memories of years she grew up on the family ranch near Hillside, AZ, and on into the hills of Nevada where she and her first husband worked for what was called "The Mighty MC". Ranching and horses were so deeply imparted to her heart that she kept the memories alive in her poetry, and kept a horse in her front yard right up to her dying day. She's no longer with us, but her poetry will keep her memory alive and give us that special insight to her way of life and loves.

BILLIE JO MCFARLAND Born in Prescott, Arizona in January of 1952, to Odis and Patsy Sullivan, she's the middle child of three, all girls. She graduated from Prescott High School, and married her cowboy husband, Mike McFarland shortly afterward. Mike attended college, but found ranch-life more to his liking, so they moved to the O RO Ranch north of their home-town, Prescott, and began her education as a cowboy's wife. "I was happy and thrilled to learn all the rules of this special life." Tradition, culture, heritage, all play a part in that education. At seventy-one he still punches cows, and I still follow him around." They've raised seven children, have 16 grandkids, and fostered several, three of which they adopted.

* BERTHA MONROE   No longer with us, Bertha grew up in the hard knock life of the working cowboy and his family. She and her husband owned and leased ranches near Camp Verde and she ran a bull-riding school and nurtured a local cowboy church there for many years. Even after they sold the ranch, her love of cattle pushed her to own a small herd of Zebu cattle, which are a miniature breed from Africa. Her property there in Camp Verde allowed for her to continue to raise cattle. She moved to Idaho in her later years for a season, but she passed away in her beloved Verde Valley.

 JANET MOORE   She was born to the life, descended from generations of cowboys. She worked beside them and married one of them. She raised seven kids who all grew up in the culture, heritage and traditions of the lifestyle of the working cowboy element. She been published in several anthologies and has two books of her own poetry. The Gail I. Gardner award recipient in 2013, she's been an invited performer at many gatherings throughout the west. "I no longer enjoy the privilege of living on a ranch; however, that life is forever in my heart and soul."

 KAY KELLEY NOWELL   Kay feels privileged to have taken part in many cowboy poetry gatherings around the country. She's been a featured poet in Elko and other notable gatherings, and even appeared on the Johnny Carson show. She treasures the friends she has made through cowboy poetry. Along with her husband, Gene, she owns Hilltop Livestock, a pre-conditioning and custom feeding operation near Alpine, Texas. They run their own Gelbvieh cow/calf herd on leased country, and she loves to day work and neighbor. Her poems are all birthed from her experiences of breaking colts working cattle, and the cowboys she's known.

* EVELYN PERKINS   A part of the well known Perkins family ranch near Chino Valley, AZ. Evelyn raised her sons in the red dust of Perkinsville and watched as each made their way into the operations of the family ranch. She wrote letters and columns for the Arizona Cattlegrower's publication, *Hooves and Horns*. A handful of those are held within the pages of this book. Sent to us by her granddaughter, Karen Perkins, they hold a rich glimpse into her life nearly a hundred years ago.

* KAREN PERKINS   Generations of the Perkins family carried on the ranching history of Perkinsville and still do today. Karen fought a long and hard battle with cancer for many years, but in 2018 the disease took over and she left two children and the life she loved. Karen was so loved by her family, her friends and her peers. A gentle soul, a beautiful artist, and accomplished writer, she left a legacy that is by only a small increment held carefully within the pages of this book.

JEAN PRESCOTT Often referred to as the song-bird of Texas, Jean enjoys a long-standing career as a singer and song writer. Her roots in the TX ranching heritage and culture are as deep as they can grow. She and her husband, Gary, make an outstanding duet, and enjoy playing and singing together at numerous poetry gatherings, music festivals, private parties and world-shaping events as well. But what she loves best is her home in Ovalo, TX and a quiet front porch visit watching her horses and cattle grazing in the "front yard."

JODY PRESLEY   She married her cowboy at the age of 15, moved to a ranch near Prescott, AZ and raised two kids on the dirt roads of   Yavapai County ranches for many years. Her wonderful sense of humor, and gutsy way of attacking life's problems gave her plenty of first hand experience in the back country and corrals of ranches in the area. She currently lives in Chino Valley, but re-lives those years in conversations and memories.

JANET MCMILLAN RIVES   Born and raised in Connecticut, she moved with her family to Tucson at age 16. Her mother's family had been living out stories of the southwest since 1902. After graduating from the University of Arizona, she left Arizona, but was drawn back to the desert as a snowbird after retiring in 2004 as a professor of economics from the University of Northern Iowa. She's read, written and loved poetry throughout her life, and has been influenced by her surroundings in New England, the Midwest, and the desert Southwest. She's been published in *Lyrical Iowa, Sandcutters, the Avocet, Unstrung and Voices from the Plains.*

DARLA JO ROBINSON Born in Prescott, Arizona, Darla grew up on the Yolo, Cross U, M Diamond and Long Meadow ranches. Her parents both played guitar and sang, which led to a family band in her school years. She played bass, her brother the drums, dad the lead guitar and mother on the rhythm guitar. She is well versed in the ways of the working cowboy, and married her cowboy husband in the early 1980s. Since then, they've raised four kids in the ways and wiles of the live-stock industry, pounding dirt in Texas, New Mexico, Arizona and Colorado.

PERILEE SHARP Raised in the rocky mountains of Yavapai County, she was following her dad to cat-tle before she started school. Half Way Camp on the Triangle HC Ranch was home until her dad passed 1979. She was responsible for plenty of horse-tracks through Burro Creek Canyon and the pine and piñon country around Camp Wood Mountain. She's stayed horseback, raised her two kids in the livestock industry, and given them a solid taste of the lifestyle, culture and the precious heritage she received from her mother and father, as well as six generations of her family tree still hooked deep in Arizona.

SHIRLEY TECKLENBURG Eighty years young at the printing of this book, she's been married to her husband Frank for sixty-seven years. She's worked as a soda jerk, school bus driver, teacher's aid, medical secretary, and as a wife and mother. She's also been a Sunday school teacher and coordinator of several Vacation Bible School ministries. She spent eighteen years on the dirt roads of Arizona, now living in Pueblo, Colorado.

HEIDI M. THOMAS Heidi grew up on a working ranch in eastern Montana, riding and gathering cattle for branding and shipping. Her parents taught her a love of books, and her grandmother rode bucking stock in rodeos. She followed her dream of writing, with a journalism degree from the University of Montana. Heidi is the author of the award-winning *Cowgirl Dreams* novel series, and Cowgirl Up: A History of Rodeo Women, as well as other fine books. She makes her home in North-Central Arizona.

FRANCES VANCE   Frances lives with her cowboy husband and three children on a ranch north of Williams, AZ. God has given her a life that delights her to her core. Life could have taken so many other turns. She traveled in Central and South America, graduated from a university with two degrees. None of those adventures have compared to that of this life as a cowboy's wife. It has been her greatest honor and pleasure

ANDREA WAITLEY   At one time she thought all ranch women dressed like Victoria Barkley and ruled with an iron hand covered in velvet. To her surprise, she married a Texas cowboy and reality set in. After the death of her cowboy poet, Larry McWhorter, she married Colorado rancher, Frank Waitley. "Larry's poetry introduced me to the romance of our Western heritage, but being married to Frank has taught me to deeply respect our Western heritage. Until one has lived it, they cannot begin to really appreciate the work and dedication it takes to get that beef to the plate.

CARROL WILLIAMS   Born in east Los Angeles in 1938, her family moved to Prescott, AZ when she turned four. As a young girl she raised goats on their farm just below Thumb Butte mountain. She dreamed of becoming a horsewoman, and in 1956 God answered her dream. She married Roy Williams, a cowman extraordinaire. Together they raised four children of their own, and any others that came along as they ranched and farmed all over Arizona. Their home-place is outside of Wickenburg where they still ranch. Her poetry and stories are based on her many ranching experiences.

JOLYN YOUNG   Jolyn lives on a remote ranch in eastern Oregon with her husband and their three kids. As a cowboy's wife, she has lived on 7 ranches in 3 different states, including the most remote cow camp in Arizona. To read her words is to visit the true life and times of the working cowboy, his peers and their families. No stranger to the hills and valleys of the West, her words will take you for a visit there.

KIP CALAHAN YOUNG   Kip was born and raised in Colorado. After high school she started playing and singing in honkytonks around the southwest area, and won Marlboro Talent Round Up in the late 80s in San Diego. She's traveled throughout the United States and did two tours in Japan. Her life on a large ranch in the southwest corner of New Mexico gave her the inspiration to write and sing cowboy songs, and won her the Rising Star Award with the Western Music Assoc. Her song, *What Cowboy Means,* was song of the year. Later she won Female Vocalist of the Year and her CD *Dust Devil Angel* won Album of the Year from the Academy of Western Music. After meeting her husband Dale they made a conscious decision to live for the Lord. Dale picked up the bass guitar and they formed Forever Young Ministry. They have now committed their lives to singing for the Lord playing traditional hymns and County Gospel Music.

203

INDEX OF AUTHORS AND TITLES
* Deceased

37129424R00117

Made in the USA
San Bernardino, CA
27 May 2019